the Edgy Veg

138
CARNIVORE-
APPROVED
VEGAN RECIPES

By Candice Hutchings

WITH JAMES AITA

Robert
ROSE

Library and Archives Canada Cataloguing in Publication

Hutchings, Candice, 1988–, author
The edgy veg: 138 carnivore-approved vegan recipes / Candice
Hutchings with James Aita.

Includes index.
ISBN 978-0-7788-0581-6 (hardcover).

1. Vegan cooking. 2. Cookbooks. I. Aita, James, 1980–, author
II. Title.

TX837 H88 2017   641.5'636   C2017-905005-2

Disclaimer
The recipes in this book have been carefully tested by our kitchen and our tasters. To the best of our knowledge, they are safe and nutritious for ordinary use and users. For those people with food or other allergies, or who have special food requirements or health issues, please read the suggested contents of each recipe carefully and determine whether or not they may create a problem for you. All recipes are used at the risk of the consumer.

We cannot be responsible for any hazards, loss or damage that may occur as a result of any recipe use.

For those with special needs, allergies, requirements or health problems, in the event of any doubt, please contact your medical adviser prior to the use of any recipe.

Cover and book design: **WALTER GREEN**
Cover and interior photography: **BRILYNN FERGUSON**
Editor: **MEREDITH DEES**
Copyeditor: **JENNIFER FOSTER**
Recipe Editor: **JENNIFER MACKENIZE**
Proofreader and indexer: **GILLIAN WATTS**
Food & Prop Styling: **CAMILLE STONE AND CANDICE HUTCHINGS**

The publisher gratefully acknowledges the financial support of our publishing program by the Government of Canada through the Canada Book Fund.

Canadä

PUBLISHED BY ROBERT ROSE INC.

120 Eglinton Avenue East, Suite 800
Toronto, Ontario, Canada M4P 1E2
Tel: (416) 322-6552
Fax: (416) 322-6936
www.robertrose.ca

Printed and bound in Canada

2 3 4 5 6 7 8 9 TCP 25 24 23 22 21 20 19 18 17

*To my Omi Renate
and Opa Albrecht
for teaching me all
my important life
lessons in the garden
and the kitchen*

Table of Contents

The Main Squeeze

On the Side

Thirsty Girl

Sweet Endings . . . or Beginnings – We Don't Judge

Acknowledgments

Index

What Is The Edgy Veg?

Hi, we're *THE EDGY VEG*, and we make the vegan food you actually want to eat. We know what you're thinking: "Not another vegan cookbook!" And we empathize, we really do. If we have to spend another day scrolling through our Instagram feed and seeing yet another pile of zucchini noodles or a meticulously decorated acai bowl staring back at us, we're going to throw ourselves out the window. We're adults, and we have needs. And these needs include, but are not limited to, a juicy burger, extra fries and a margarita to wash it all down. You can't eat a kale salad every day, after all.

Congrats, you've managed to find the one vegan (and one plant-based enthusiast) in a world of quinoa and kale who refuses to go with the grain. That's a pun, get it? Quinoa . . . it's a grain. You better get used to these types of eye-rolling dad jokes, because this book is full of them!

This journey to becoming an Edgy Veg began nine years ago. I (Hi, I'm Candice!) saw a poster in the subway with the headline "Why love one but eat the other?" sandwiched by a photo of a puppy on one side and a piglet on the other. I won't get into the hairy (get it . . . animals?) details, but I gobbled down one last Jamaican patty, said my goodbyes and never looked back. Okay, that's not entirely true — it was more for dramatic effect. I tried to never look back, but I had a hard time surviving on leafy salads and handfuls of nuts, which is what all the other vegans seemed to be eating. How does anyone eat like that — for life? The result: frequent hangry evenings ordering, canceling, reordering and canceling pizza deliveries. I was frustrated. Why should I have to give up my insatiable need for comfort food just because I wanted to eat better for myself, animals and the planet? This question changed the course of my future (and later, James's!) forever.

Within the first three months of becoming vegan, I missed a lot of the foods that had previously brought me comfort. It became apparent to me right away that I needed suitable substitutes. In order to manage this whole vegan thing, I decided to teach myself to cook and create the vegan food I wanted. I quickly learned that there was no need to reinvent the wheel. I could use traditional flavor profiles and techniques with plant-based substitutions to achieve something just as delicious. Hey, who was I to argue with the Anthony Bourdains of the world? One evening watching *Julie & Julia*, accompanied by a bottle of wine, I had an epiphany: "I can do that!!!" Enter: The Edgy Veg.

We are 50 percent vegan mad scientist and 50 percent former carnivore food snob — how's that for an A-Team? When James came on the scene, he was a connoisseur of French food and a lush for stinky cheese. To him, vegan food was a "crazy" concept, and I was deter-mined to prove him wrong — and I continued to prove him wrong for two years before he officially came over to the dark side. Fist pump! Now we explore the possibilities of the alternative food world together. James challenges me with meat- and cheese-centric meals, and I rip my hair out trying to veganize them.

The Edgy Veg is a food movement. We create recipes that will satisfy all dietary philosophies. Every single one of our recipes must receive our signature carnivore-approved blessing and we wouldn't serve a meal that a meat-eater wouldn't enjoy devouring. We are on a journey to revolutionize the food we define as "vegan." Instead of only salads, soba noodles, smoothies, tempeh and tofu, we repurpose familiar favorites. We get off on recreating a feeling of nostalgia by veganizing our childhood cravings, fast-food faves and food-nerd obsessions, which is exactly what you'll find in this book. These pages are filled with meaningful recipes that have inspired us over the years and have been tirelessly tested on friends and family.

Now it's your turn: help us repave what the world defines as vegan food. Toss out the dairy, milk, eggs and hemp seeds and say hello to tasty tacos, perfect pizza and an indulgent Veggs Benny breakfast that you — and your tastebuds — can feel good about. Put down that spiralizer and get ready to have your cake, burgers and fries, and EAT THEM, TOO!

Candice & James

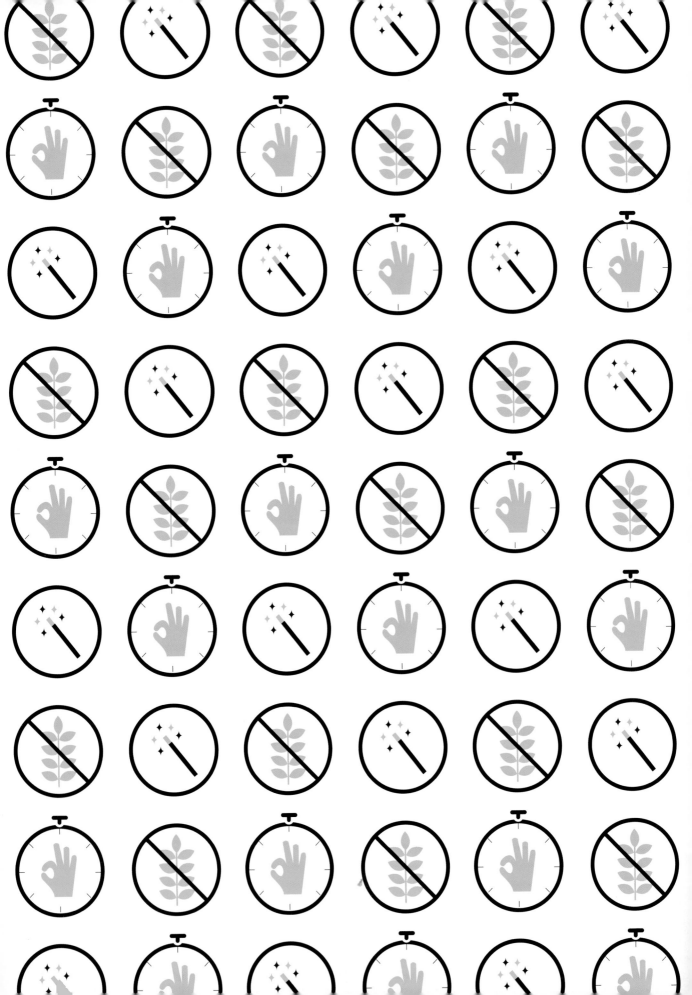

The Essentials

How to Use This Book

Whether you're a long-time vegan, a new vegan, a vegetarian, a dairy-free flexitarian or not vegan at all, this book is for you. The pages are filled with all the things I wish someone had told me when I first went vegan and started to cook (and they would have saved me many nights of guiltily eating pizza in my closet). All the recipes can be easily matched with each other to create full meals, and they are designed so you can experiment with combinations (fun!). Here is everything you need to make the food you love, the vegan way — even if you've never cooked before. (Pro tip: If you've never cooked before, a bottle of wine can always help you get through the recipe and your guests through the meal. Just kidding; I believe in you!) Before hopping into your cooking journey, make sure you read the recipe. Yeah, I know, what a weird thing to say, but trust me, you'll save yourself a ton of anxiety if you read the whole recipe from start to finish. For example, you may need to refer to another recipe that has a different cooking time or use some weird cooking contraption. Since preparedness is close to godliness, I'm telling you to READ THE RECIPE FIRST! Aside from a few fan favorites that can be found on our YouTube channel and website, this book is packed with brand-new, exclusive-to-this-book-only recipes that we hope will help enrich your love for plant-based, compassionate cooking. Enjoy.

Icons

There are three icons in this book. They look like this:

Gluten-Free: Are you celiac or do you just like to stay away from gluten? *I swear, we're not judging.* Then these recipes are for you. Make sure you swap out the soy sauce for tamari if we didn't clarify it in the recipe (but you knew that already, didn't you?).

Quick and Easy: These recipes take 45 minutes or less to prepare, which is great for when your mother-in-law calls to announce a visit on her way over to your apartment.

Great for Entertaining: Make more friends and influence people with these crowd-pleasers. They are tried and true, and the only reason people like us.

Hack It!

These are great tips to change up the recipe if you've tried it before or you feel like getting adventurous. I've hid tons of great little Easter eggs in these sections, like alternative ingredients, sauces and flavor twists, and I even let you know how long the dish will keep in the fridge or freezer so you can keep savoring the taste. (*Pro tip*: Read this section before the recipe to get your inspiration flowing.)

How-To Videos

Are you a visual learner? Do you have ADHD, like I do? Do you like additional nuances and hacks? Are you addicted to the Internet? Do you just miss me? Perfect! Head over to the YouTube channel (▶ youtube.com/edgyveg/) on your mobile device or laptop (make sure to protect them if you're in the kitchen). I cover many of the basics, plus I'll keep you company for emotional support while you're waiting for your seitan to cook.

Share Proudly

This book isn't about us, it's about you. *You go, Glen Coco.* Proudly share your creations with us and the rest of the community — we love seeing what you come up with. Use the hashtag **#edgyvegcookbook** on Twitter and Instagram (feel free to tag **@edgyveg #edgyveg**) and you might even get featured!

Trolling the Vegans

One of the most fun things about having a YouTube channel is getting to play with Internet trolls. Ahh, I love the Internet. It also means that I've heard every interesting question, joke, myth and jab about veganism. Let's take a moment and address some of these for the purpose of this book, shall we?

Q: Why eat vegan?

Do you like being nice to animals? What about breathing clean air? Do you enjoying living on this marble in the sky we call Earth? Cool! Eat more plant-based, vegan food because it's good for you, the animals and the environment. Seriously! More than 56 billion farmed animals are killed every year by humans for food. Avoiding animal products is one of the easiest ways you can take a stand against animal cruelty and exploitation. By adopting a vegan diet, you can personally save up to 100 animals a year and thousands during your lifetime.

Why not save the planet while you're at it?! Meat and other animal-product production places a heavy burden on our planet. The crops and water required to feed, transport and process the animals, not to mention the amount of grain required for meat production, substantially impact deforestation and are one of the main contributors to climate change. One of the most effective things you can do to lower your carbon footprint is to avoid all animal products and eat these recipes, instead.

Don't care about the planet or those pesky animals? Well, I'm sure you care about yourself, and a vegan diet is super good for you! According to the Academy of Nutrition and Dietetics, eating a plant-based diet means you are less likely to develop heart disease, cancer, diabetes or high blood pressure — many of the leading causes of death in the United States. It is also one of the best lifestyles for increased energy, younger-looking skin and maintaining a healthy body weight for a long period of time.

Q: Where do you get your protein?

Don't sweat it! I get all the protein I need from fruits, vegetables, legumes and leafy greens. If gorillas and elephants can thrive on plant-based protein, you can, too! But if you're really that worried about it, go get yourself a vegan protein powder.

S: Vegan food is boring!

Nuh-uh! Just take a look through the pages of this book you're holding. Anything you can eat, I can eat vegan. And trust me, it will be just as satisfying.

S: Vegan cheese and meat suck!

Let's all get on the same page here: vegan cheese and meat 100 percent *used to* suck. But food manufacturers and culinary wizards have been working tirelessly to create flawless substitutions for cheese mongers just like you. You can see our fan faves in the Easy Substitutions section (page 24).

Q: I'll give this a try, but where can I buy . . . x?

Most of the ingredients found in this book can be purchased at large supermarkets, and anything else can usually be found at a local wellness or health food store. Edgy Veg tip: I order tons of stuff online cuz I'm lazy.

S: I want to know more.

Don't believe what I'm saying? Here's a list of books and movies created by people much smarter than I am talking about these very issues.

BOOKS TO READ

- *Eating Animals* by Jonathan Safran Foer
- *Farm Sanctuary: Changing Hearts and Minds about Animals and Food* by Gene Baur

- *My Beef with Meat* by Rip Esselstyn
- *Skinny Bitch* and *Skinny Bastard* by Rory Freedman and Kim Barnouin
- *The 30-Day Vegan Challenge* by Colleen Patrick-Goudreau
- *The China Study* by T. Colin Campbell and Thomas M. Campbell II
- *The Engine 2 Diet* by Rip Esselstyn
- *The World Peace Diet* by Will Tuttle

THINGS TO WATCH

- BBC's *Carnage*
- *Cowspiracy*
- *Earthlings*
- *Farm to Fridge*
- *Food, Inc.*
- *Forks over Knives*
- *Hungry for Change*
- *The Engine 2 Diet*
- *The Ghosts in Our Machine*
- *Vegucated*

Tools of the Trade

Arguably, one of the best parts about cooking is all the toys you get to shop for to make it easier on yourself. Both James and I are not allowed in kitchen stores anymore because of our inability to control our shopping goblins. To help calm *your* shopping goblins, I've provided a handy list of the items you actually need versus the ones that you can get away with purchasing later, after your wallet has recovered. However, I can't guarantee this list will stop you from getting that $1,500 copper blender once you've seen it . . .

CRITICAL

- Baking sheets
- Blender, preferably high-powered
- Can opener
- Citrus juicer
- Colander
- Corkscrew
- Cutting boards (at least two)
- Deep-fry thermometer
- Electric hand mixer
- Fine-mesh sieve
- Knives: chef's, paring and bread
- Large cast-iron skillet
- Mason jars in a variety of sizes
- Measuring cups and spoons
- Mixing bowls (S, M, L)
- Parchment paper
- Pastry brush
- Rolling pin
- Sauce pans (S, M, L)
- Skillets (S, M, L)
- Slotted spoon
- Spatulas and wooden spoons
- Stock pots (we recommend two)
- Tongs
- Whisk

IMPORTANT

- Coffee or spice grinder
- Food processor
- 9- by 5-inch (23 by 12.5 cm) and 8- by 4-inch (20 by 10 cm) metal loaf pans
- Microplane-style zester
- 9-inch (23 cm) spring-form pans
- Wire cooling racks

HELPFUL

- Mortar and pestle
- Pastry cloth
- Stand mixer
- Toaster oven

Pantry Staples

I'm not sure that you can call our situation a "pantry" — our kitchen supplies are scattered in and above cupboards, on shelves and on counters both in our kitchen and in our office, which doubles as a studio-equipment storage unit. That said, cooking vegan does require a few key stock items. Keep these on hand, and you'll never go hungry.

GRAINS

- Brown rice
- Basmati rice
- Dried bread crumbs
- Large-flake (old-fashioned) rolled oats
- Panko bread crumbs
- Pasta of all shapes and sizes. Macaroni and spaghetti are a great place to start.
- Quinoa
- Unbleached all-purpose flour (or gluten-free all-purpose if you're celiac)
- White bread flour
- White rice

NUTS AND SEEDS

- Ground flax seeds
- Raw unsalted almonds
- Raw unsalted cashews
- Raw sunflower seeds
- White sesame seeds

CANNED GOODS

- Black beans
- Chickpeas (the source of aquafaba!)
- Kidney beans
- Pinto beans
- Plum (Roma) tomatoes, stewed, diced, whole — just get them all
- Vegetable bouillon cubes/powder or vegetable Better Than Bouillon Seasoned Vegetable Base for broth. (Homemade is always best, but if you're short on time, the quickest and cheapest way to make broth is by mixing hot water and vegetable bouillon.)

SWEETENERS

- Agave nectar
- Coconut sugar
- Light brown sugar (yellow sugar in Canada)
- Organic confectioner's (icing) sugar
- Organic white sugar
- Pure maple syrup
- Superfine sugar (Hack It!: Make your own superfine sugar at home by placing organic white sugar in a food processor or blender and pulsing until it reaches a fine, but not powdery, consistency.)

Some refined sugars are processed using bone char. Look out for words like "organic," "unrefined," "fair trade" or "vegan" on the package, which will make shopping for sweeteners a lot easier.

SPECIALTY AND BAKING

- A variety of dried mushrooms (I like porcini, shiitake and portobello.)
- Baking powder
- Baking soda
- Dairy-free/vegan dark chocolate chips
- Food-grade matcha (unless you're doing a tea ceremony, you don't need the expensive stuff.)

- Nutritional yeast
- Pure vanilla extract

HERBS AND SPICES

- Bay leaves
- Black salt (also known as *kala namak*)
- Cayenne pepper
- Curry powder
- Dried basil
- Dried dill
- Dried oregano
- Dried marjoram
- Dried rosemary
- Dried thyme
- Dry mustard powder
- Freshly ground black pepper
- Garam masala
- Garlic powder
- Ground cinnamon and cinnamon sticks
- Ground ginger
- Ground nutmeg
- Hot paprika
- Onion powder
- Paprika
- Red pepper flakes
- Sea salt (I prefer pink Himalayan)
- Sweet Hungarian paprika
- Whole cloves
- Whole and ground cumin

EGG REPLACERS

(See the substitution section to learn more about each ingredient.)

- Ener-G egg replacer
- Ground flax seeds
- The Vegg Vegan Egg Yolk powder

VEGAN MEAT SUBSTITUTES

(See the substitution section to learn more about each ingredient and how to use it.)

- A variety of frozen pre-pared varieties
- Firm tofu
- Texturized vegetable pro-tein (TVP)
- Vital wheat gluten (I make seitan with this stuff)

VEGAN NON-DAIRY PRODUCTS

(See the substitution section to learn more about each ingredient.)

- Almond milk
- Canned full-fat coconut milk
- Soy milk
- Vegan cheese shreds
- Vegan cheese slices
- Vegan Parmesan
- Vegan soy- or almond-based cream cheese
- Vegan soy-based sour cream

SEED AND NUT BUTTERS

- Natural and conventional peanut butter
- Tahini

OILS AND VINEGARS

- Apple cider vinegar
- Asian spicy chile oil
- Balsamic vinegar
- Coconut oil
- Olive oil for cooking and extra virgin olive oil for salad dressing

- Peanut oil
- Red and white wine vinegars
- Rice vinegar
- Toasted sesame oil
- Vegetable oil (I prefer sunflower)
- White vinegar

SAUCES

- Cayenne pepper sauce (like Frank's RedHot)
- Hoisin sauce
- Liquid smoke
- Mirin
- Red and white wine (okay, it's not a sauce, but it's very important for flavor)
- Shaoxing wine
- Soy sauce or gluten-free tamari
- Sriracha sauce
- Vegan Worcestershire (I like The Wizard's)
- White and brown miso paste

Easy Substitutions

The real trick to vegan cooking is substitutions, and the good news is that there's only a handful of them, so get to know this section really well. Are you in the bookstore right now? Read this section and then put the book back. (No, just kidding. My publisher will kill me for saying that!)

Egg Substitutions

In vegan baking, one of the hardest things to mimic is the function of an egg. Luckily, there isn't a lot of baking in this book! Yahoo! Nonetheless, here are my favorite vegan egg substitutes.

Flax Egg: Flax eggs are used in baking for structure and texture. For each egg, combine 1 tbsp (15 mL) ground flax seeds with 3 tbsp (45 mL) water. Mix with a fork and place in the fridge to set for 15 minutes.

Powdered Egg Replacer (I like Ener-G): A store-bought combination of potato starch, tapioca starch and leavening agents. It can be used in all baked goods and many dishes that call for eggs as "glue" for breading or to help a batter/cake/loaf hold its shape — things like batters, pâtés — you feel me. Mix 1-1/2 tsp (7 mL) Ener-G with 2 tbsp (30 mL) water.

The Vegg Vegan Egg Yolk: A powder that simulates the taste and texture of egg yolks.

Use it in any dish that calls for eggs or egg yolks. It's great for Ritzy Hollandaise (page 53) or Peanut Butter and Jam French Toast (page 66), as a glaze for baked goods and even just to dip your toast into. To make 2 yolks: In a blender, blend 1 tsp (5 mL) Vegg powder with 1/4 cup (60 mL) water on High until gelatinous.

Aquafaba: That liquid hiding in your can of chickpeas can be whipped like egg whites into meringues or replace eggs entirely in baking. Who knew!? Three tbsp (45 mL) aquafaba is equivalent to 1 whole egg, and 2 tbsp (30 mL) is equivalent to about 1 egg white. If using as a binding agent for batters to hold their shape, lightly whip the liquid until foamy. As an egg white meringue, whip for 15 minutes, until peaks form. Use on lemon meringue pie or in chocolate mousse and even icing.

Meat Substitutes

Vital wheat gluten: A natural protein found in wheat that I use to make homemade seitan.

Seitan: A fantastic vegan meat substitute also known as "wheat meat," which has been a staple in China and other parts of Asia since the sixth century! It easily mocks the texture and taste of beef or chicken.

Tofu: Haters, drop your pitchforks. All "bad" tofu is simply prepared by someone who doesn't know what they're doing. Tofu is a versatile, low-calorie protein that will easily take on the flavor of any dressing, marinade or sauce, making it a perfect meat substitute that's readily available. Bonus: it also works wonders in sauces, baking and dips. Try our Ritzy Hollandaise (page 53) or New York Cheesecake with Raspberry Coulis (page 254).

Textured Vegetable Protein (aka TVP): TVP is inexpensive and easy to use. It's made of dehydrated soy and for your convenience comes minced or in chunks in a variety of shapes and sizes. It works well to replace any meat, including ground beef, stewing beef and chicken strips — all you need is a good marinade.

Ditch the Dairy

While I have a couple cheese sauce recipes in this book that are fantastic, sometimes you need the flavor of American, Cheddar or mozzarella. Veganism has become such a popular food trend, and food manufacturers have taken notice. In many groceries stores you can find the basic dairy substitutions such as soy and almond milk, as well as veganaise, vegan margarine and, if you're lucky enough to live in an urban center, vegan American cheese slices, veggie Parmesan and more. I have a fantastic blog post called **"The Best Vegan Substitutions"** (http://www.theedgyveg. com/2017/06/14/the-best-vegan-substitutions/), where I list all our favorite brands. Here are some substitution guidelines to follow if you're new to the whole vegan cooking scene.

Milks

Unsweetened Soy Milk: Soy milk has the most protein of all the non-dairy milks available. Soy milk is stable at high temperatures, and is a stellar dairy replacement for sauces, baking and dredging and in batters. It is rich and creamy, but it also has a strong nutty flavor that I love, personally, but is often too strong for some. For these reasons, I like to use soy milk the most in cooking.

Unsweetened Almond Milk: Almond milk is the most popular non-dairy milk of choice for those looking to cut down on their dairy consumption. It can be used in place of cow's milk in any recipe, but it has almost no protein, making it less stable and less creamy compared to unsweetened soy. Due to its mild and subtle flavor, it's a delicious cow's-milk replacement in coffee and smoothies and over cereal.

Coconut Milk: There is a big difference between the coconut milk beverage from a carton and coconut milk from a can. Be sure to take note of which one is called for in a recipe. In this book, we use full-fat coconut milk from a can exclusively. The coconut milk beverage from a carton is delicious when added to coffee, smoothies, creamy soups or cereal. It also works well in oatmeal and in some cooking and baking. However, coconut milk from a can is much thicker and creamier and is great for curries and sauces, and it is thick enough to whip into whipped cream or to use in homemade ice cream.

Other

Nutritional Yeast (aka Nooch): Not to be confused with brewer's yeast or active yeast used for baking, nutritional yeast is an inactive form of yeast that is yellow in color. It has a nutty and almost cheesy flavor that is perfect for making homemade cheese. You can also sprinkle it on salads or pastas. Find it in most health food stores and in the health food section of many well-stocked grocery stores.

Vegan Butter: You can use any dairy-free non-hydrogenated margarine, which can be found at many local grocery stores. Many are accidentally vegan and not that difficult to find. If you have access to it, Earth Balance Buttery (spread or sticks) is our gold standard. It tastes JUST like salty, buttery heaven and is essential in many dishes that require that signature butter flavor. We use it a lot.

Yogurt: There is a wide variety of nut-, soy- and coconut-based yogurts available. They are becoming available in large chain grocery stores and are always available at your local health food store. We use them interchangeably.

Ice Cream: There are so many new vegan ice cream options! I get so excited to see vegan ice cream made from tofu, almond milk, cashews, coconut and even beans. We both prefer tofu- and cashew-based ice creams because they are the creamiest and most authentic compared to the real deal. If you want to join the fun of making ice cream at home (and become slightly obsessed like I am), check out the three ice cream recipes (pages 267 to 271) in the dessert section of this book!

HOW TO SOAK CASHEWS
You'll notice that I ask you to soak cashews all over the place in this book — it's the basic building block for almost all creams. If you've never done this before, here's how: In a medium bowl or mason jar, combine cashews and water to cover; let soak overnight. Drain cashews using a fine-mesh sieve and rinse well. If you don't have time to soak your nuts overnight, pour boiling water over cashews to cover them and soak for 1 hour.

Hack It!

If you're allergic to cashews, substitute raw almonds. If you're allergic to all nuts, use raw sunflower seeds.

And that, my friends is the who, what, when, where and, most important, the reason why I am so passionate about your vegan journey. I hope you enjoy each and every recipe that fills these pages as much as I do, and don't forget to find the time to laugh a little along the way. All right — let's get cooking already!

#Basic(s)

/ˈbāsik/   *adjective*

1. forming an essential foundation or starting point; fundamental.

noun

1. (plural) the essential facts or principles of a subject or skill • *Learning the basics of cooking.*

2. someone who conforms to their surroundings and claims they are unique, often drinking pumpkin spice lattes (#PSL) and low-calorie margaritas, posting selfies on social network sites daily and using irrelevant hashtags • *"Becky is so basic. She goes grocery shopping in her yoga pants, even if she's not going spinning that day. She also says she's gluten free, but then posts soooo many photos of avocado toast. Like, I love all my friends, but I secretly hate her right now."*

WHILE BASICS MIGHT BE BORING, uninspiring and devoid of defining characteristics that make food interesting to the naked eye, they provide the foundation to make wonderful, beautiful creations, worthy of unique and interesting hashtags.

Pizzeria-Style Dough

MAKES 4 THIN-CRUST PIZZAS (SERVES 6 TO 8)

Pizza has always been there for me. It selflessly fed me after long nights of studying (read: partying), soothed every broken heart in my twenties and now acts like a vehicle for consuming wine and smooth jazz and building friendships in my (soon-to-be) thirties. Pizza never tells me no, and it will always be my first true love.

1. In a food processor, combine flour, sugar, sea salt and yeast; pulse 5 times until well incorporated. Add water, olive oil, red pepper flakes and oregano; mix for 30 seconds until the ingredients form a ball that rides around in the bowl — fun!

2. Transfer dough to a lightly floured surface and knead a couple of times by hand until a smooth ball forms. You'll know the dough is ready when you cut off a small piece about the size of a golf ball and it stretches very thin without breaking or tearing. If the dough tears, the gluten isn't quite ready; knead for 2 more minutes.

3. Divide dough into four even pieces and place each in a bowl; cover with plastic wrap (or place in separate freezer bags). Let rise in the fridge for at least 5 hours or up to 1 day (recommended).

4. Remove dough from fridge 1 hour before baking and let come to room temperature.

5. Place your pizza stone in the oven and preheat to 500°F (260°C). (If you don't have a pizza stone, use a round baking sheet and cook for 8 to 12 minutes.)

6. One ball at a time, transfer dough to a floured surface and stretch out by hand as much as possible. Using a rolling pin, work from the middle of dough outward and flatten to 1/4 inch (0.5 cm) thick. Place dough on pizza stone and bake on the bottom rack of preheated oven for 2 minutes.

7. Remove crust from oven, leaving the stone in oven, and top with your favorite sauce, toppings and vegan cheese of choice. Bake for 6 to 10 minutes until browned on top and crispy on the bottom and cheese is melted but not burned. Try our Perfectly Pleasing Pesto Pizza (page 154).

FOOD PROCESSOR
PIZZA STONE (OPTIONAL)
ROLLING PIN

3 cups white bread flour 750 mL
1 tbsp organic sugar 15 mL
1 tsp sea salt 5 mL
1-1/4 tsp quick-rising (instant) yeast 6 mL
1 cup water 250 mL
1-1/2 tbsp olive oil 22 mL
1/2 tsp red pepper flakes 2 mL
1/2 tsp dried oregano 2 mL
Additional white bread flour for kneading

Foolproof Gnocchi

I enjoy the masochistic satisfaction of homemade pasta making. I spent my first few years in Germany, where the women in my family slaved over pots of boiling water making späetzle with a device that looked like a medieval torture tool for poorly behaved children. Sure, you could just go and buy a box of premade potato noodles, just like you could also buy a fake Louis Vuitton handbag, but we both know there's no satisfaction in that faux lifestyle.

1. Arrange potatoes on a prepared baking sheet and bake in preheated oven for 1 hour.

2. Holding a clean tea towel in one hand and a fork in the other, pick up a hot potato with the fork and place in your other hand (the one with the towel). Scrape out the potato flesh into a large bowl, discarding the skins. Using a food mill, ricer or fork, mash potato to get rid of any clumps.

3. Using a spoon, spread out potato pile until it forms an even 1/2-inch (1 cm) to 1-inch (2.5 cm) layer in the bowl. (This will help cool down the potato.) Let cool for about five minutes. It should be just cool enough that no steam is coming off it.

4. Sprinkle 1 cup (250 mL) flour over potato. Using a pastry blender or fork, combine flour until you no longer see white from the flour and the potato starts to look like dough. Using a fork, spread out dough in an even 1/2-inch (1 cm) to 1-inch (2.5 cm) layer. Sprinkle 1/2 cup (125 mL) flour overtop and combine using pastry blender or fork.

5. Once flour has been incorporated, using your hands, start forming a ball with the dough. Place dough onto work surface and sprinkle with 1/2 cup (125 mL) flour. Fold the dough in half and press to combine; repeat until dough has sucked up all the flour and becomes slightly sticky. DO NOT knead.

6. When it starts sticking to your hands, form the dough into a rectangular loaf about 4 inches (10 cm) wide. Sprinkle dough with a bit of flour and rub gently to coat; set aside. Clean work surface well.

7. Bring a large pot of salted water to a boil.

8. Cut loaf crosswise into 8 to 10 1-inch (2.5 cm) pieces. Using your palms, roll them into 1-1/2 inch (4 cm) long "snakes." Sprinkle flour over snakes and roll to prevent stickiness.

PREHEAT OVEN TO 350°F (180°C)
BAKING SHEET LINED WITH PARCHMENT PAPER
FOOD MILL OR RICER (OPTIONAL)
PASTRY BLENDER (OPTIONAL)

4 large yellow-flesh potatoes, cut in half lengthwise 4
2 cups unbleached all-purpose flour, sifted and divided 500 mL
Additional unbleached all-purpose flour

9. Using a very sharp knife, cut snakes into 1/2-inch (1 cm) pieces. In batches, drop gnocchi into boiling water and cook for 3 to 5 minutes, until gnocchi start to float to the top. Be ready with a slotted spoon to catch them as they float.

10. **To serve immediately:** Transfer to a large skillet if you're cooking in a butter sauce or saucepan for anything more substantial (read: saucy) and cook over medium-high heat for about 3 to 5 minutes, until heated through. **To save for later:** Place cooked gnocchi in an ice bath, drain and store in a container in the fridge for up to 5 days.

~~~ HACK IT! ~~~

To freeze gnocchi: Arrange uncooked pasta in a single layer on a baking sheet lined with parchment paper and place in the freezer until solid. Place frozen gnocchi into a freezer bag and keep for up to 6 weeks. To reheat, remove gnocchi from freezer and transfer directly to boiling water. Increase cooking time by 1 to 2 minutes and proceed with recipe.

All You Need Is Broth

MAKES 6 CUPS (1.5 L)

Here's the thing about store-bought vegetable broth — it tastes like liquid hate. But not the *Waiting to Exhale*, light-your-cheating-husband's-car-on-fire kind of passion. Store-bought vegetable broth tastes like a sad Gigi from *He's Just Not That Into You*, who just happened to be in the neighborhood to return her first date's pen. My oma used to tell me that anything homemade is always made with love, and couldn't we all use a bit more of that?

1. In a large stock pot, heat olive oil over medium-high heat. Add onion, celery, carrots, mushrooms, tomatoes, garlic, ginger, rosemary, parsley and salt; sweat, stirring occasionally, for 10 to 15 minutes, until vegetables begin to soften and brown lightly.

2. Add water, bay leaves and peppercorns and bring to a boil. Immediately reduce heat to low and simmer for 1 to 1-1/2 hours, until the liquid has reduced by half. Taste along the way, and salt if you need to.

3. Strain through a fine-mesh sieve into another large pot, bowl or mason jar, discarding solids. Let cool completely; cover and refrigerate for up to 5 days or freeze for up to 3 months.

 *HACK IT!*

Sweating your veg helps them develop sweeter flavors with more complexity. This is the most important step.

The more finely you chop your veggies, the more flavorful your broth will taste.

FINE-MESH SIEVE

3 tbsp olive oil 45 mL
1 large white onion, unpeeled, roughly chopped 1
10 celery stalks, roughly chopped 10
4 large carrots, roughly chopped 4
2 cups cremini or button mushrooms, roughly chopped 500 mL
3 tomatoes, halved 3
1 garlic head, roughly chopped 1
1 1/2-inch (1 cm) piece fresh ginger, roughly chopped 1
2 sprigs fresh rosemary 2
1/4 cup sprigs fresh flat-leaf (Italian) parsley 60 mL
1 tsp salt (approx.) 5 mL
12 cups water 3 L
2 bay leaves 2
1 tsp whole black peppercorns 5 mL

Eggcellent Eggless Dip

MAKES THE EQUIVALENT OF 4 EGGS

Real talk: All food tastes better when it's coated in a thick, crunchy breading. James made it perfectly clear early on in our relationship that my breading wasn't fooling anyone — it needed a thicker, eggier binding. After dipping many foods in many liquids, we finally have a worthy go-to, and we go to it often. Use this eggless dip for any recipe that calls for dredging and frying — it'll change your life. #NotClickBait

1. In a mug or small bowl or measuring cup, combine 3 tbsp (45 mL) soy milk and cornstarch. Mix until smooth.

2. In a small saucepan, heat 1 cup (250 mL) soy milk over medium-high heat, whisking constantly, until steaming, but not boiling. Reduce heat to medium low.

3. Slowly, whisking constantly, pour in cornstarch mixture. Cook for 5 to 7 minutes, whisking constantly, until it thickens to the consistency of whipped eggs. Transfer to a shallow bowl and let cool slightly.

1 cup + 3 tbsp unsweetened soy milk, divided 295 mL
1 tbsp cornstarch 15 mL

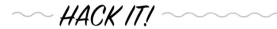

HACK IT!

This is the perfect egg wash for breading and frying. It is wonderfully thick and perfectly replicates real eggs.

Store Eggcellent Eggless Dip in the fridge for up to 3 days.

Better Than Eggs: Tofu Scramble

SERVES 2

Tofu has always been a hard sell to non-vegans. I remember the first time I offered to make James an all-vegan brunch. He said that he liked me, but he didn't really like tofu. I immediately heard Meatloaf singing in my head, "I would do anything for love . . . but I won't do that." After his first bite, his tune quickly changed to "I believe in miracles. Where you from, you sexy thing?"

1. In a small bowl or blender, combine nutritional yeast, garlic powder, turmeric, black salt, pepper, bouillon powder and water. Whisk or blend until smooth. Set aside.

2. In a medium skillet, heat coconut oil over medium-high heat. Add onion and sauté for about 3 minutes, until translucent. Add tofu and cook for 5 minutes, stirring occasionally, until most of the moisture from the tofu has evaporated.

3. Add nutritional yeast mixture to the pan and cook, without stirring, for 4 minutes, until the liquid has reduced by half. Continue to cook, stirring occasionally, for 5 to 8 minutes, until the liquid has evaporated and the tofu begins to stick to the bottom of the skillet. Serve with a side of vegan bacon (pages 45 to 48), toast and fresh fruit for a yummy high-protein breakfast.

BLENDER (OPTIONAL)

3 tbsp nutritional yeast 45 mL
2 tsp garlic powder 10 mL
1/4 tsp ground turmeric 1 mL
1/2 tsp black salt or sea salt 2 mL
1/2 tsp freshly ground black pepper (approx.) 2 mL
1/2 tsp vegetable bouillon powder 2 mL
1/2 cup water 125 mL
1 tbsp coconut oil 15 mL
1 small onion, finely chopped 1
1 package (16 oz/450 g) medium tofu, crumbled 1

～ HACK IT! ～

Black salt or *kala namak* is a naturally sulfuric salt that mimics the taste and smell of eggs. I always have it on hand to replace that eggy flavor in egg-free cooking.

Throw in your favorite chopped veggies for some crunch in Step 2. My favorite combo is 1/2 cup (125 mL) chopped kale and 1/2 cup (125 mL) chopped mushrooms. Yummy!

Add shredded vegan cheese to the pan in the last 5 to 8 minutes of cooking for a cheesy, salty twist.

Into Tex-Mex? Add 1/4 cup (60 mL) salsa and a finely chopped jalapeño to the pan in the last 5 to 8 minutes of cooking for a spicy kick.

It's a Bella Mozzarella

MAKES ABOUT 1 CUP (250 ML)

What's a pizza without some beautiful melty, mouth-watering cheese on it? More to the point, how does one expect to survive without being able to have cheesy veal parmigiana (page 173) or gooey grilled cheese in their life? So go forth and melt away, because, well, cheese.

1. In a blender, combine cashews, water, tapioca starch, nutritional yeast, coconut oil, lemon juice, garlic powder, onion powder and sea salt. Blend on High until smooth. (Do not be concerned about how wet and thin it looks, we're going to cook this down.)

2. In a small saucepan, cook cashew mixture over medium-high heat, whisking constantly, for about 5 minutes, until the mixture begins to thicken and bubbles. Immediately remove from heat and transfer to a container. Place in the fridge for a minimum of 3 hours before using. Use in any recipe that calls for melted mozzarella.

1/2 cup raw cashews, soaked overnight and rinsed (see page 26) 125 mL
3/4 cup water 175 mL
1/4 cup tapioca starch 60 mL
2 tbsp nutritional yeast 30 mL
1 tbsp coconut oil 15 mL
1 tsp freshly squeezed lemon juice 5 mL
1/4 tsp garlic powder 1 mL
1/4 tsp onion powder 1 mL
1 tsp sea salt 5 mL

 *HACK IT!*

I like to use this on our Perfectly Pleasing Pesto Pizza (page 154) or spread it on bread for our Très Flawless French Onion Soup (page 94).

Store covered mozzarella in the fridge for up to 7 days.

Become a Master of Seitan: Chicken

SERVES 6

My first attempt at seitan was sometime in 2010. I was young and foolish, and thought gluten flour was just regular flour with gluten in it. *Oh, the horror!* Trust me, I will never forget that soggy dumpling mess. So much for "adulting." When done correctly — with the appropriate flour — this seitan flawlessly mocks the juicy, mouth-watering texture of meat. It's James's fave.

1. In a large bowl, combine 1 cup (250 mL) wheat gluten, sea salt, nutritional yeast, onion powder and poultry seasoning; whisk to combine.

2. In another large bowl, combine vegetable broth and tahini; whisk until smooth. Using a spatula, carefully fold wheat gluten mixture into vegetable broth mixture until combined. (You might need to use your hands for this.)

3. Sprinkle work surface with 1 tbsp (15 mL) vital wheat gluten. Knead the dough until it's elastic but not dry. Add additional wheat gluten if dough feels too sticky and knead some more. To make chicken breast cutlets, see page 39. To make burgers or schnitzel, see page 39.

1 cup + 1 tbsp vital wheat gluten, divided (approx.) 265 mL
1/2 tsp sea salt 2 mL
2 tbsp nutritional yeast 30 mL
1 tsp onion powder 5 mL
1/2 tsp poultry seasoning 2 mL
3/4 cup All You Need Is Broth (page 34) 175 mL
1/4 cup tahini 60 mL

～～ HACK IT! ～～

Trust me, poultry seasoning is vegan.

Add chicken seitan to any recipe that calls for chicken strips or pieces, such as stir-fries, pizza or sandwiches. Thinly slice chicken breasts or cut into bite-size chunks or 2- to 3-inch (5 to 7.5 cm) strips.

Try chicken seitan in our Italian Bakery Veal Parmigiana (page 173), Why So Syrian Chicken and Rice (page 158), In Search of General Tso's Chicken (page 162) or Famous Edgy Veg Fried Chicken (page 174).

Chicken Breasts

1. Complete the Become a Master of Seitan: Chicken recipe.

2. Form dough into 2 chicken breast–size loaves. Place one piece of aluminum foil larger than the loaves in front of you horizontally. Place another piece of aluminum foil overtop vertically. Place 1 loaf in the center of each piece of foil and roll up tightly, twisting up the ends like a wrapped candy. Make sure everything is tightly packed. Move wrapped loaves to a baking sheet and bake in preheated oven for 1 hour, rotating the loaves every 20 minutes for even cooking. Poke each loaf with spoon: it should feel very, very firm when it's done.

3. Remove from oven and let wrapped loaves cool completely for about 45 minutes on a wire rack. Use as a substitute in any recipes that call for chicken.

PREHEAT OVEN TO 350°F (180°C)

Chicken Burgers or Schnitzel

1. Complete the Become a Master of Seitan: Chicken recipe.

2. Divide dough into 6 small burgers or divide into 8 equal pieces and roll out into 1/2-inch (1 cm) schnitzel cutlets. (Keep in mind they will grow to be about twice their size, so make them smaller than you would normally.) Place burgers or schnitzel in a Dutch oven and cover completely with vegetable broth. Cover and cook in preheated oven for 1 hour, flipping seitan after 45 minutes. Remove burgers or schnitzel from broth and let cool for about 45 minutes on a wire rack. Use as a substitute in any recipes that call for chicken burgers or schnitzel. These taste the best when they are breaded, baked or fried (like the Chick-Fillet Deluxe, page 213).

PREHEAT OVEN TO 350°F (180°C)

4 cups All You Need Is Broth (page 34) 1 L

HACK IT!

To freeze: Wrap each cooked breast, burger or schnitzel separately in plastic wrap and place in a freezer bag or container. Freeze for up to 3 months. Thaw in the fridge overnight, prior to use.

Seitan Mastery 2.0: Beef

SERVES 6

Seitan is a form of vegan wizardry that easily imitates the texture and taste of beef. With just a few switch-ups and a couple of key, flavorful ingredients, you've got vegan steak, stir-fry meat or veggie stewing beef. No wand or incantation necessary.

PREHEAT OVEN TO 350°F (180°C)
FOOD PROCESSOR

1. In a large skillet, heat olive oil over high heat. Add mushrooms and sauté for 5 minutes, stirring constantly, or until slightly browned and tender. Set aside.

2. In a large bowl, whisk together vital wheat gluten, nutritional yeast, brown sugar, garlic powder, onion powder, turmeric, parsley, thyme and salt. Set aside.

3. In a food processor, combine vegetable broth, mushrooms, soy sauce, mustard, tahini, BBQ sauce, liquid smoke, garlic and pepper; pulse until mushrooms are finely chopped.

4. Slowly pour vegetable stock mixture into vital wheat gluten mixture and knead with your hands. The mixture should be dough-like and not overly sticky. Add more wheat gluten if dough feels too sticky and knead some more. Form into a log and place on a plate. Let stand for 5 to 10 minutes on top of preheating oven.

5. Meanwhile, place one piece of aluminum foil horizontally in front of you. Place another piece of aluminum foil vertically overtop. (You'll be able to wrap the whole log in foil.) Place log in center of foil and roll it up tightly, twisting up the ends like a wrapped candy. Move the wrapped log to a baking sheet and bake in preheated oven for 1 to 1-1/2 hours. Rotate log every 20 minutes for even cooking, and poke with a spoon after 1 hour to test the firmness. It should feel very, very firm when it's done. If it's not done after 1 hour, poke for firmness every 15 minutes for up to 1-1/2 hours total.

6. Remove from oven and let wrapped log cool on a wire rack for about 15 minutes, until you can handle it with your hands.

Ingredients:

- 2 tbsp olive oil 30 mL
- 2 cups cremini mushrooms 500 mL
- 1-1/2 cups vital wheat gluten (approx.) 375 mL
- 1/4 cup nutritional yeast 60 mL
- 2 tbsp packed brown sugar 30 mL
- 1 tsp garlic powder 5 mL
- 1 tsp onion powder 5 mL
- 1/2 tsp ground turmeric 2 mL
- 1 tbsp dried parsley 15 mL
- 1/2 tsp dried thyme 2 mL
- 1/2 tsp salt 2 mL
- 3/4 cup All You Need Is Broth (page 34) 175 mL
- 1 tbsp soy sauce 15 mL
- 1 tbsp Dijon mustard 15 mL
- 1/4 cup tahini 60 mL
- 1/4 cup vegan-friendly BBQ sauce 60 mL
- 1 tsp liquid smoke 5 mL
- 2 garlic cloves, minced 2
- 1/4 tsp freshly ground black pepper 1 mL

7. Unwrap and slice crosswise 1 inch (2.5 cm) thick for steaks, paper-thin slices for sandwiches or bite-size chunks for stir-fries.

HACK IT!

If you have access to a meat slicer, I highly recommend slicing at least half of this roast very thin and using it in sandwiches.

Add a meaty texture to soups and stews by cutting this roast into bite-size chunks.

To make homemade veggie dogs and sausages: Prepare through Step 3. Roll into many tiny sausages, wrap individually and proceed with recipe, cooking for 40 minutes to 1 hour, until very firm.

To make minced beef: After Step 6, cut seitan log into chunks and place in a food processor. Process until seitan resembles ground hamburger meat.

To freeze: Wrap each cooked log in plastic wrap and place in a freezer bag or container. Freeze for up to 3 months. Thaw in the fridge overnight prior to use.

Neat Balls, Bro

MAKES ABOUT 18 BALLS

No one can resist my neat balls. People have told me that my neat balls are very tender and flavorful. There's nothing like a neat ball, except for maybe fragrant spiced nuts (page 127). Okay, all jokes aside, the texture of these meatballs is perfect. We make a large batch, freeze half and keep them for lazy Sunday night spaghetti dinners.

1. In a small saucepan, bring rice and water to a boil. Reduce heat to low, cover with a tight-fitting lid and cook according to package instructions. (Most brown rice cooks in 30 to 40 minutes.) Remove from heat, drain any excess water and let stand, covered, for 5 minutes. Measure out 1/2 cup (125 mL) cooked rice and set aside. Place leftover rice in the fridge for fried rice or brown rice bowls, for up to 3 days.

2. In a food processor, process onion and garlic until finely chopped. Set aside.

3. In food processor, pulse eggplant until chopped. Set aside.

4. In a large skillet, heat 1 tbsp (15 mL) olive oil over medium heat. Add onion and garlic and cook for about 5 minutes, stirring occasionally, until soft and translucent. Add mushrooms and eggplant, cover and cook for 5 minutes, until mushrooms are soft and have released their juices. Remove cover and cook, stirring occasionally, for about 10 minutes, until most of the liquid has evaporated. Remove from heat and let cool to the touch.

5. Using a pastry brush, brush parchment paper with 1/2 tbsp (7 mL) olive oil.

6. In a large bowl, combine parsley, flax seeds, oregano, thyme, cumin, red pepper flakes, 3/4 cup (175 mL) bread crumbs, cooked brown rice, sea salt and pepper. Add eggplant mixture and combine, using a wooden spoon or your hands. Add an additional 1/4 cup (60 mL) bread crumbs if the mixture is too sticky.

7. Using your hands, form 1-1/2-inch (4 cm) balls with eggplant mixture and place on prepared baking sheet. Brush balls with remaining 1/2 tbsp (7 mL) olive oil and bake in preheated oven for 30 minutes, until they begin to brown slightly. Remove from oven and enjoy alongside pasta, in a meatball sub or on their own.

PREHEAT OVEN TO 400°F
(200°C)
FOOD PROCESSOR
BAKING SHEET LINED WITH
PARCHMENT PAPER

1/2 cup brown rice, rinsed 125 mL

1/2 cup water 125 mL

1 small onion, chopped 1

4 garlic cloves, crushed 4

1 large eggplant, peeled and cut into large chunks 1

2 tbsp olive oil, divided 30 mL

2 cups diced portobello mushrooms 500 mL

1 cup chopped flat-leaf (Italian) parsley 250 mL

3 tbsp ground flax seeds 45 mL

1 tsp dried oregano 5 mL

1 tsp dried thyme 5 mL

1/2 tsp ground cumin 2 mL

1/2 tsp red pepper flakes 2 mL

3/4 to 1 cup dried bread crumbs 175 to 250 mL

1/2 tsp sea salt 2 mL

1/2 tsp freshly ground black pepper 2 mL

BACON, THO
(Bacon 4 Ways)

This recipe is dedicated to every Internet troll who's ever commented "BACON" (yup, in all caps) on any vegan recipe I post. I mean, I get it; bacon is just one of those foods recovering omnivores will never get over. Well, friends, I think I have the answer: four delicious vegan bacons that aren't a complete disappointment. Is it bacon? No. Is it salty, sweet, smoky and completely delicious in a BLT? Oh, heck, yes!

Smoky Marinade

MAKES 1 CUP (250 ML)

Make this marinade then choose your "meat." Easy, peasy.

1. In a medium bowl, combine soy sauce, maple syrup, liquid smoke, if using, olive oil, apple cider vinegar, nutritional yeast, paprika and pepper. Use on bacon right away or store in the fridge for up to 5 days. Leftover marinade can be frozen for up to 1 month.

1/4 cup soy sauce or tamari 60 mL
1/4 cup pure maple syrup 60 mL
1/4 tsp liquid smoke (optional) 1 mL
3 tbsp olive oil 45 mL
3 tbsp apple cider vinegar 45 mL
2 tbsp nutritional yeast 30 mL
1 tsp smoked paprika 5 mL
Freshly ground black pepper

Coconut Bacon

MAKES 5 CUPS (1.25 L) BACON BITS

This is perfect for sprinkling on sandwiches, salads and even desserts.

1. In a large bowl, combine marinade and coconut; toss to coat. Let stand, tossing occasionally, for about 30 minutes, until coconut has absorbed marinade.

2. Spread out coconut flakes evenly on prepared baking sheet and bake in preheated oven for 20 minutes, flipping every 5 minutes, until dark in color and resembling the texture of crumbled bacon. Make sure to watch very carefully and flip coconut to minimize the likelihood of burning.

3. Transfer to a bowl, large plate or another baking sheet immediately, so it does not continue to cook and burn. Let cool completely. Store in a container in the fridge for up to 2 weeks.

> PREHEAT OVEN TO 325°F (160°C)
> BAKING SHEET LINED WITH PARCHMENT PAPER OR GREASED WITH COCONUT OIL

1 recipe Smoky Marinade (above) 1
5 cups flaked unsweetened coconut 1.25 L

Mushroom Bacon

MAKES 15 TO 20 SLICES

We love this bacon in savory dishes like pastas, on burgers and sprinkled on top of veggies like Brussels sprouts and baked potatoes.

1. In a large bowl, combine marinade and mushrooms; toss well to coat. Let stand for 15 minutes, tossing every 5 minutes to distribute marinade.

2. Arrange mushrooms in a single layer on prepared baking sheet and bake in preheated oven for about 15 minutes, until mushrooms begin to brown. Flip and continue to bake for about 15 minutes more, until browned.

3. Remove from oven and let cool for 10 minutes, until mushrooms harden slightly and become crispy like bacon. Store in a container in the fridge for up to 5 days.

PREHEAT OVEN TO 325°F (160°C)
BAKING SHEET LINED WITH PARCHMENT PAPER

1 recipe Smoky Marinade (page 46) 1
4 king oyster mushrooms, thinly sliced lengthwise 4

Rice Paper Bacon

MAKES ABOUT 22 SLICES

This veggie bacon is the closest replica of traditional breakfast bacon yet. Alongside tofu scramble and pancakes, it's the breakfast of champions.

1. Using a very sharp pair of scissors, cut rice paper into 1-inch (2.5 cm) strips, similar to bacon. (The rice paper will crack a bit, but sharper scissors should eliminate major breakage. If you are having a lot of trouble with cracking, simply brush rice paper with a bit of water to soften before cutting.)

2. Pour water into a measuring cup.

3. Take two strips of rice paper of similar shape and lay them side by side. Using a pastry brush, brush the top of each sheet with water and stack them one on top of the other. They should start to stick together. Brush water along the outsides of the fused strips and lay fused strips on a piece of parchment or cutting board. Repeat process until you run out of space or rice paper.

4. Using a dry pastry brush (do not use the one you used for water — it will dilute the sauce), brush marinade onto one side of one fused rice paper strip. Lay strip marinade side down on prepared baking sheet. Brush marinade on top, coating generously. Repeat with remaining fused strips, whisking marinade every so often to prevent separation.

5. Bake in preheated oven for about 7 to 8 minutes, until browned and crisp. The strips burn easily, so keep an eye on them and remove bacon from baking sheet immediately once it's finished cooking. Store in a container at room temperature for up to 3 days or in the fridge for 2 weeks.

PREHEAT OVEN TO 400°F (200°C)
2 BAKING SHEETS LINED WITH PARCHMENT PAPER

5 9-inch (23 cm) rice paper wrappers 5
2 cups water 500 mL
1 recipe Smoky Marinade (page 46) 1

Eggplant Bacon

MAKES 40 SLICES

This bacon takes the most time to prepare of our bacon recipes, but it makes a wonderfully meaty substitute for bacon in any pasta, salad or sandwich when you want a bit more oomph.

1. Cut eggplant into quarters lengthwise, then slice each quarter into thin 1/4-inch (0.5 cm) lengthwise slices.

2. Transfer to a large colander and sprinkle with salt, in layers. Let stand for 30 minutes to 1 hour to draw out the moisture.

3. Rinse eggplant with water and pat dry. In a large bowl, combine eggplant slices and marinade; stir gently to coat. Let stand for 1 hour, stirring every 15 minutes to recoat.

4. Preheat oven to 250°F (120°C).

5. Arrange eggplant slices on baking sheets in a single layer. Bake in preheated oven for roughly 1 to 1-1/2 hours, until eggplant is dry, golden brown and slightly crispy (it will crisp more as it cools). Store in a container at room temperature for up to 3 days or in the fridge for up to 2 weeks.

2 BAKING SHEETS LINED WITH PARCHMENT PAPER AND BRUSHED LIGHTLY WITH OLIVE OIL

2 **eggplants,** peeled 2
1 **tbsp** salt 15 mL
1 **recipe** Smoky Marinade (page 46) 1

Essential Non-Dairy Cream

MAKES 2 CUPS (500 ML)

Homemade cashew cream was one of the first vegan staples I learned how to make when I went vegan in 2010. It flawlessly helped me ditch the dairy in my cooking. With this base you can make almost anything creamy, like Burrito-Worthy Sour Cream (page 51). Wherever heavy cream once stood in your omni repertoire, cashew cream resides now.

1. In a medium bowl or mason jar, combine cashews and water to cover; let soak overnight. Drain cashews, using a fine-mesh sieve, and rinse well.

2. In a blender, combine cashews and 3/4 cup (175 mL) water. Blend on High until super smooth and creamy, stopping the motor to scrape down the sides of the container as necessary. It should resemble sour cream. Add more water, 1 tbsp (15 mL) at a time, if blender has trouble blending or if cream is too thick. Use immediately or transfer to a mason jar or container and keep in the fridge for up to 5 days.

FINE-MESH SIEVE
HIGH-POWERED BLENDER

2 cups raw cashews 500 mL
Water

 *HACK IT!*

If you don't have time to soak your nuts overnight, pour boiling water over cashews to cover them and soak for 1 hour.

Add more water to create a half-and-half-style cream.

For a sweeter variation, add 2 tbsp (30 mL) pure maple syrup and 1/2 tsp (2 mL) vanilla extract while blending. Use this sweet variety to top desserts or fruit.

Hell No! Egg-Free Mayo

MAKES ABOUT 1 CUP (250 ML)

There are two types of people in this world: mayo lovers and those who call it "the devil's condiment." I sit proudly in camp number one. As a kid, I used to eat mayo by the spoonful — no sandwich or potato salad required. While those days are behind me, I do enjoy this egg-free version on burgers and use it as a french-fry dip with reckless abandon.

1. In a coffee mug or other tall cup that fits an immersion blender, combine aquafaba, chickpeas, lemon juice, apple cider vinegar, mustard powder and garlic powder. Blend until completely smooth.

2. With blender running, slowly drizzle in grapeseed oil in 2 to 3 tbsp (30 to 45 mL) amounts. Blend without adding oil for a few seconds, then continue drizzling. The mixture will become thick and creamy. Depending on the brand of grapeseed oil, thickening can happen with 3/4 to 1 cup (175 to 250 mL) oil. Season to taste with black salt and continue mixing, until salt is incorporated and mayo is whipped. Use immediately or transfer to a small mason jar or container and keep in the fridge for up to a week.

IMMERSION BLENDER

3 tbsp aquafaba 45 mL
1 tbsp canned or cooked chickpeas, drained and rinsed 15 mL
1 tbsp freshly squeezed lemon juice 15 mL
1 tsp apple cider vinegar 5 mL
1/4 tsp dry mustard powder 1 mL
1/4 tsp garlic powder 1 mL
3/4 cup to 1 cup grapeseed oil 175 to 250 mL
Black salt or sea salt

~~ HACK IT! ~~

Aquafaba means bean water. The easiest way to get it is to drain a can of chickpeas. Instant egg whites!

Black salt or *kala namak* is a highly sulfuric-tasting (and smelling) salt from Indian volcanic rock. It gives a lovely egg-like flavor to any dish you add it to.

Add 1 tsp (5 mL) pure maple syrup or agave nectar, 1/4 tsp (1 mL) onion powder and a pinch of paprika in Step 1 to get a more Miracle Whip–like flavor.

Mix in 1 tsp (5 mL) powdered wasabi at the end for a spicy kick.

Burrito-Worthy Sour Cream

We always have a mason jar of this stuff on hand, given the amount of Tex-Mex consumed in our home. Without it, your burrito would just be #Sad.

1. In a blender, combine cashews, water, apple cider vinegar, lemon juice and salt. Blend on High until smooth, scraping down the sides of the blender as needed. Taste and add more lemon juice and water, as necessary, until it resembles the taste and texture of sour cream. Use immediately or transfer to a mason jar or container and store in the fridge for up to 1 week.

 *HACK IT!*

Turn this into a creamy salsa dip by whisking 3/4 cup (175 mL) chunky salsa and a finely chopped jalapeño into sour cream.

HIGH-POWERED BLENDER

1-1/2 cups raw cashews, soaked overnight and rinsed (see page 26) 375 mL

1/2 cup water (approx.) 125 mL

1 to 2 tsp apple cider vinegar 5 to 10 mL

3 tbsp freshly squeezed lemon juice (approx.) 45 mL

1/4 tsp salt 1 mL

The Art of Cheese Sauce

MAKES ABOUT 3-1/2 CUPS (875 ML)

At age five, young James pushed aside a bowl of boxed mac and cheese made by his loving cousin. He looked up at her and said, "It's not real cheese." Ladies and gentlemen, the critic I work with on a daily basis. I am happy to report that this cheese sauce has never been pushed aside, and seconds are always requested — especially when used on nachos.

1. In a small saucepan, combine potato and carrots; cover with water and bring to a boil over high heat. Reduce heat to medium and boil gently for about 20 minutes, until soft.

2. Using a colander, drain carrots and potato over a small bowl, reserving the liquid. Set aside liquid.

3. In a blender, combine potato, carrots and soy milk. Blend on High until very smooth. Add olive oil, salt, lemon juice, nutritional yeast, tapioca starch, onion powder, garlic powder, mustard powder and paprika; blend until very smooth. Add reserved liquid, as necessary, until the consistency resembles cheese sauce.

4. Season to taste with salt and cayenne pepper, if using.

~~ HACK IT! ~~

Turn this recipe into a queso dip by thinning it out with an additional 1/4 cup (60 mL) reserved liquid or unsweetened soy milk and mixing in a diced small tomato and a finely chopped jalapeño or green chiles.

This is a very versatile sauce that can be used in mac and cheese, nachos or even jalapeño poppers (page 124).

BLENDER

1 large potato, peeled and cubed 1
2 large carrots, peeled and chopped 2
1/4 cup unsweetened soy milk 60 mL
2 tbsp olive oil 30 mL
1 tsp salt 5 mL
1-1/2 tsp freshly squeezed lemon juice 7 mL
1/4 cup nutritional yeast 60 mL
1 tbsp tapioca starch 15 mL
1/4 tsp onion powder 1 mL
1/2 tsp garlic powder 2 mL
1/2 tsp dry mustard powder 2 mL
1/2 tsp paprika 2 mL
Salt
Cayenne pepper (optional)

Ritzy Hollandaise

MAKES 1-1/2 CUPS (375 ML)

The epitome of brunch sophistication is a perfect hollandaise, which can be found at the Ritz in Paris. I've managed to crack the secret to this rich, creamy, lemony butter dream of a sauce so you can enjoy it at home, no passport required. I guarantee even the French would approve.

1. In a blender, combine almond milk, tofu, black salt, nutritional yeast, mustard powder and turmeric. Blend on High until smooth. Add lemon juice and blend until smooth. Add cayenne and pepper; pulse until well combined.

2. Remove the plug in the lid. While the blender is running, slowly add vegan butter through the hole in the lid and blend until smooth. Check the taste and consistency of hollandaise and adjust salt, pepper and lemon juice, if necessary.

 *HACK IT!*

To ensure that the butter does not separate from the rest of the sauce, you want to make sure that you are adding melted vegan butter at a comically slow pace. If you think you're pouring slowly, go even slower.

Hollandaise is a very versatile sauce; it's stellar in our Veggs Benny (page 70), but also tastes fabulous on top of our Better Than Eggs: Tofu Scramble (page 36), in The All-Day Breakfast Sandwich (page 73), drizzled over veggies or even as a dip for Potatoes Served in the French Manner (page 224).

The hollandaise sauce will keep for 5 days in the fridge and for 1 month in the freezer. It can easily be reheated on days that you're feeling extra lazy. To reheat, whisk in a small saucepan over low heat for about 5 minutes, until heated through.

BLENDER

1/2 cup unsweetened almond milk 125 mL

1/2 cup soft silken tofu 125 mL

1/2 tsp black salt or sea salt 2 mL

2 tbsp nutritional yeast 30 mL

1/4 tsp dry mustard powder 1 mL

1/4 tsp ground turmeric 1 mL

1-1/2 tbsp freshly squeezed lemon juice (approx.) 22 mL

1/4 tsp cayenne pepper 1 mL

1/4 tsp freshly ground black pepper 1 mL

1/3 cup vegan butter, melted 75 mL

Presto, Pesto

MAKES 1-1/4 CUPS (300 ML)

Pesto is the quickest and easiest sauce to make, and it can take any meal from drab to fab. When I was in university, I literally put the stuff on everything: pasta, salad and personal-size pita pizzas. When it comes to sauces, pesto is the besto.

1. In a food processor, combine basil, sunflower seeds, garlic and nutritional yeast; process until a coarse meal forms.

2. Slowly add 1/4 cup (60 mL) olive oil in a steady drizzle through the feed tube as you pulse. Process until it forms a smooth paste. Add more olive oil, if necessary, if the mixture is too dry. You want the pesto to be moist and spreadable. Season with sea salt to taste.

HACK IT!

Add a handful of other fresh herbs for a fun flavor twist. Mint and oregano are my personal faves.

Store in the fridge for 5 to 7 days or in the freezer for up to 3 months.

FOOD PROCESSOR

2 cups loosely packed fresh basil 500 mL
1/2 cup raw sunflower seeds 125 mL
2 garlic cloves 2
3 tbsp nutritional yeast 45 mL
1/4 to 1/2 cup olive oil 60 to 125 mL
Sea salt

Weekend at Béarnaise

MAKES ABOUT 2 CUPS (500 ML)

Béarnaise sauce comes from the hollandaise family, but is laced with white wine vinegar and tarragon. We like to call it "man sauce." It may appear to be rich and delicate, but it's actually rugged and macho, and it pairs perfectly with our succulent portobello steak (page 158) — a recipe we created especially for all the men out there (they won't even notice it's mushrooms. Wink.)

1. In a small saucepan, melt vegan butter over medium-low heat. Set aside.

2. In another small saucepan, combine white wine vinegar, white wine, shallot and half of the tarragon. Simmer over medium heat for about 15 minutes, stirring occasionally, until the liquid has reduced to about 2 tbsp (30 mL). Strain the liquid through a fine-mesh sieve into a blender, discarding solids. Set aside saucepan.

3. Add nutritional yeast, tofu and turmeric to blender. Blend on High until smooth. With the blender running, slowly add melted vegan butter through the hole in the lid until well incorporated. Season with black salt.

4. Transfer the mixture back to the small saucepan and heat over low heat, whisking vigorously and constantly, until mixture is thickened and resembles a traditional béarnaise sauce. Stir in the remaining chopped tarragon and parsley, and set aside to thicken slightly, about 5 minutes.

FINE-MESH SIEVE
BLENDER

1 **cup** vegan butter 250 mL
1/4 **cup** white wine vinegar 60 mL
3 **tbsp** dry white wine 45 mL
1 **shallot,** minced 1
2 **sprigs** fresh tarragon, chopped and divided 2
1/3 **cup** nutritional yeast 75 mL
2/3 **cup** soft silken tofu, drained 150 mL
1/4 **tsp** ground turmeric 1 mL
1/4 **tsp** black salt 1 mL
1 **sprig** flat-leaf (Italian) parsley 1

～ HACK IT! ～

Black salt is what makes this recipe more "eggy." If you can't find it, use sea salt instead.

One of the most common mistakes people make while preparing a béarnaise is to add the butter too quickly. Add vegan butter at a rate that may seem unnaturally slow.

Drizzle over roasted vegetables, such as asparagus, broccoli or zucchini, for an haute cuisine feel.

Store in the fridge for up to 3 days. To reheat, whisk in a small saucepan over low heat for about 5 minutes, until heated through.

Liquid Gold Gravy

MAKES 1-1/2 CUPS (375 ML)

Most foods are just vehicles for consuming sauce. And of all the options, a killer gravy reigns supreme. It bestows a soothing, hominess to anything it touches, like a warm, savory embrace that fixes all wrongs. Did you screw up your dinner? No problem — just throw some gravy on it!

1. In a medium skillet, melt 3 tbsp (45 mL) vegan butter over medium heat. Add shallot and sauté for about 3 minutes, until translucent. Add mushrooms and cook for about 8 minutes, until slightly browned. Add 2 cups (500 mL) water, bouillon powder and soy sauce. Bring to a boil over high heat. Boil until mixture is reduced by one-fifth; add wine. Boil for about 15 minutes, until reduced by one-third.

2. Meanwhile, in a small bowl, combine cornstarch and 3 tbsp (45 mL) water.

3. Add the remaining vegan butter to skillet, 1 tbsp (15 mL) at a time, whisking constantly, until melted. Reduce heat to medium-low. Add cornstarch mixture, 1 tbsp (15 mL) at a time, whisking constantly, until thick.

1/3 cup vegan butter, divided 75 mL
1 shallot, minced 1
1 cup chopped cremini mushrooms 250 mL
Water
2 tsp vegetarian bouillon powder 10 mL
1 tbsp soy sauce or tamari 15 mL
1/4 cup dry red wine 60 mL
1 tbsp cornstarch 15 mL

 ## HACK IT!

Omit the cornstarch to make a dippable and drippy jus, which is perfect for Le Dip Français (page 196)!

Enjoy this gravy on top of Potatoes Served in the French Manner (page 224) or with schnitzel (page 173), or serve alongside a Thanksgiving feast.

Store leftovers in a container and keep in the fridge for up to 1 week. To reheat, whisk in a small saucepan over medium heat for 5 to 8 minutes, until heated through.

Marinara Italiano

MAKES ROUGHLY 2-3/4 CUPS (675 ML)

As far as I'm concerned, there is never a reason to buy premade marinara sauce. Like a family secret, this recipe has been in my back pocket for years whenever I need a quick crowd-pleaser that wows with minimal effort. Congratulations! You are well on your way to becoming the Italian *nonna* you always wanted to be.

FOOD PROCESSOR

1 **can** (28 oz/796 mL) crushed tomatoes 1
1/3 **cup** tomato paste 75 mL
1/4 **cup** flat-leaf (Italian) parsley, chopped 60 mL
2 **garlic** cloves, crushed 2
1 **tsp** dried oregano 5 mL
3 **tbsp** extra virgin olive oil 45 mL
1 **small** onion, finely chopped 1
Sea salt
Freshly ground black pepper

1. In a food processor, combine tomatoes, tomato paste, parsley, garlic and oregano. Pulse until well incorporated.

2. In a medium saucepan, heat olive oil over medium heat. Sauté onion for about 3 minutes, until fragrant and translucent. Add the tomato mixture and bring to a boil. Immediately reduce heat to low, cover and simmer, stirring occasionally, for 40 minutes or until slightly reduced and thickened. Add sea salt and pepper to taste. Serve with Foolproof Gnocchi (page 32), Spaghetti and Neat Balls, Bro (page 166), or Italian Bakery Veal Parmigiana (page 173).

HACK IT!

If you don't want to use canned tomatoes, use 4 cups (1 L) chopped fresh Roma tomatoes instead.

Give this sauce a spicy kick by adding 1/2 tsp (2 mL) crushed red pepper flakes in Step 2.

Store in the fridge for up to 1 week or freeze for up to 3 months.

HOLY AIOLI!

Holy moly, that's a lot of aioli! No matter what you're cookin' up, I've got your dippin' and spreadin' covered.

Spicy

MAKES ABOUT 1/2 CUP (125 ML)

This quick and easy mayo with a li'l kick is a great accompaniment for sushi, burgers and sandwiches.

1/2 cup Hell No! Egg-Free Mayo (page 50) 125 mL
2 tbsp Sriracha sauce 30 mL
1 tsp freshly squeezed lime juice 5 mL

1. In a small bowl, combine mayo, Sriracha sauce and lime juice. Whisk until well combined. Use immediately or transfer to a mason jar or container and store in the fridge for up to 1 week.

Avocado & Chile

MAKES ABOUT 1 CUP (250 ML)

Want a creamy dip with a hint of spice that is perfect for smearing on sandwiches, burgers and tacos and as a dip for chips or jalapeño poppers (page 124)? Look no further!

MINI FOOD PROCESSOR

1/2 cup Hell No! Egg-Free Mayo (page 50) 125 mL
1/2 ripe avocado, cubed 1/2
1 tbsp freshly squeezed lime juice 15 mL
1/4 tsp red pepper flakes 1 mL
2 tbsp chopped fresh cilantro 30 mL
Sea salt

1. In a mini food processor, combine mayo, avocado, lime juice and red pepper flakes; process until combined. Transfer to a small bowl and whisk in cilantro and sea salt to taste. Use immediately.

Herbed

MAKES ABOUT 3/4 CUP (175 ML)

The easiest way to change up your mayo is to throw in your favorite herbs! This brightly flavored mayo is perfect for dipping fresh summer veggies.

1/2 cup Hell No! Egg-Free Mayo (page 50) 125 mL
1 tbsp finely chopped fresh dill 15 mL
1 tbsp finely chopped fresh flat-leaf (Italian) parsley 15 mL
1 tbsp finely chopped fresh chives 15 mL
1 tbsp finely chopped fresh tarragon 15 mL

1. In a small bowl, combine mayo, dill, parsley, chives and tarragon. Whisk until well combined. Use immediately or transfer to a mason jar or container and store in the fridge for up to 1 week.

Sun-Dried Tomato

MAKES ABOUT 3/4 CUP (175 ML)

This sweet and salty aioli is fabulous on sandwiches or as a dip for potato chips.

MINI FOOD PROCESSOR

1/2 cup Hell No! Egg-Free Mayo (page 50) 125 mL
1/4 cup oil-packed sun-dried tomatoes, drained 60 mL
1 garlic clove, coarsely chopped 1
1 tsp freshly squeezed lemon juice 5 mL

1. In a mini food processor, combine mayo, sun-dried tomatoes, garlic and lemon juice; process until smooth. Use immediately or transfer to a mason jar or container and store in the fridge for up to 1 week.

Catalan-Style

MAKES ABOUT 2/3 CUP (150 ML)

This is a spicy garlic sauce that pairs flawlessly with rice or roasted vegetables.

MORTAR AND PESTLE OR MINI FOOD PROCESSOR

2 garlic cloves, coarsely chopped 2
1/4 tsp coarse sea salt (approx.) 1 mL
1/2 cup Hell No! Egg-Free Mayo (page 50) 125 mL
1 tbsp olive oil 15 mL
1 tbsp freshly squeezed lemon juice 15 mL

1. Using a mortar and pestle, combine garlic and sea salt; mash until a paste begins to form.

2. Transfer to a small bowl. Whisk in mayo, olive oil and lemon juice. Season with additional sea salt to taste, if necessary. Use immediately or transfer to a mason jar or container and store in the fridge for up to 1 week.

Smoked Paprika

MAKES ABOUT 1/2 CUP (125 ML)

Call the fire department, cuz this dip is smokin'! Give your burgers and sandwiches a little extra something with this bad boy.

MINI FOOD PROCESSOR

1/2 cup Hell No! Egg-Free Mayo (page 50) 125 mL
1 garlic clove, coarsely chopped 1
1 tsp hot smoked paprika 5 mL
1 tsp freshly squeezed lemon juice 5 mL
Sea salt

1. In a mini food processor, combine mayo, garlic, paprika and lemon juice; process until combined. Add sea salt to taste. Use immediately or transfer to a mason jar or container and store in the fridge for up to 1 week.

Brunch

THE HANGOVER STORY

/brən(t)SH/ *noun*

1. a late-morning meal combining both breakfast and lunch. • *"It's noon; I'm meeting Chester and Muffy for brunch in Soho."*

2. a weekend meal among friends designed specifically to combat the effects of a hangover, with carbs drowned in sauces and superfluous fruit garnishes (as if you're actually going to eat the fruit). Brunch is never eaten before noon and is customarily paired with Bloody Marys and many mimosas. • *"OMG, Ashley, you won't BELIEVE what happened last night; let's go for brunch! I so need a vat of hollandaise and mimosas in my life right now."*

BRUNCH IS WITHOUT A DOUBT MY FAVORITE MEAL. The food in this chapter is designed to make you feel better about your choices from the night before while you recollect said activities with your closest confidantes. No one deserves to feel shame before noon.

The Pancake Guide

There are many ways to say, "I love you." My personal favorite is through a mile-high stack of fluffy pancakes. It doesn't matter if I'm just feeling extra affectionate, need the garbage taken out or want to build a quick bridge between arguments — pancakes will always get me the result I'm looking for.

OG Pancakes

SERVES 2

1. Set your griddle to medium heat, if using.

2. In a large bowl, combine flour, sugar, baking powder and salt.

3. In a small bowl, whisk together soy milk and apple cider vinegar. Set aside for 10 minutes. This will turn the soy milk into non-dairy buttermilk!

4. Add 2 tbsp (30 mL) coconut oil to flour mixture; whisk to combine.

5. Pour buttermilk into flour mixture; whisk until smooth.

6. Heat the griddle or a large skillet over medium heat. Add 1-1/2 tsp (7 mL) coconut oil and heat. Scoop 1/4 cup (60 mL) batter onto cooking surface for each pancake, depending on the size of your griddle or skillet (you can cook 3 to 4 at a time). Cook for 3 minutes, until you notice the bubbles have stopped opening and closing. Flip pancakes carefully. Cook for about 3 minutes, until golden brown and cooked through. Remove from heat. Repeat with the remaining batter and coconut oil. Drizzle with maple syrup.

ELECTRIC GRIDDLE OR LARGE NONSTICK SKILLET

1 cup unbleached all-purpose flour 250 mL
1 tbsp organic sugar 15 mL
2 tbsp baking powder 30 mL
1/4 tsp salt 1 mL
1 cup unsweetened soy or almond milk 250 mL
1 tbsp apple cider vinegar 15 mL
3 tbsp softened coconut oil, divided 45 mL
Pure maple syrup

Banana Chocolate Pancakes

SERVES 2

1. In a medium bowl, combine flour, baking powder and salt.

2. In a large bowl, whisk together soy milk and apple cider vinegar. Set aside for 10 minutes. This will turn the soy milk into non-dairy buttermilk!

3. Add vanilla and bananas to buttermilk; whisk until combined.

4. Add 2 tbsp (30 mL) coconut oil to flour mixture and whisk until well combined.

5. Pour flour mixture into banana mixture. Add chocolate chips; mix until combined.

6. Heat the griddle or a large skillet over medium heat. Add 1-1/2 tsp (7 mL) coconut oil and heat. Scoop 1/4 cup (60 mL) batter onto cooking surface for each pancake, depending on the size of your griddle or skillet (you can cook 3 to 4 at a time). Cook for 3 minutes, until you notice the bubbles have stopped opening and closing. Flip pancakes carefully. Cook for about 3 minutes, until golden brown and cooked through. Remove from heat. Repeat with the remaining batter and coconut oil. Serve with coconut flakes and sliced bananas, if using, and a drizzle of maple syrup.

ELECTRIC GRIDDLE OR LARGE NONSTICK SKILLET

1-1/4 cups unbleached all-purpose flour 300 mL
2 tbsp baking powder 30 mL
1/4 tsp salt 1 mL
1 cup unsweetened soy or almond milk 250 mL
1 tbsp apple cider vinegar 15 mL
1/2 tsp vanilla extract 2 mL
2 very ripe bananas, mashed 2
3 tbsp softened coconut oil, divided 45 mL
1/2 cup vegan dark chocolate chips 125 mL
Coconut flakes (optional)
Banana slices (optional)
Pure maple syrup

Peanut Butter and Baileys Pancakes

SERVES 2

1. In a large bowl, combine flour, sugar, baking powder and salt.

2. In a small bowl, whisk together soy milk, Baileys, vanilla and peanut butter.

3. Pour milk mixture into flour mixture and mix until smooth.

4. Heat the griddle or a large skillet over medium heat. Add 1-1/2 tsp (7 mL) coconut oil and heat. Scoop 1/4 cup (60 mL) batter onto cooking surface for each pancake, depending on the size of your griddle or skillet (you can cook 3 to 4 at a time). Cook for 3 minutes, until you notice the bubbles have stopped opening and closing. Flip pancakes carefully. Cook for about 3 minutes, until golden brown and cooked through. Remove from heat. Repeat with the remaining batter and coconut oil.

5. Top with chantilly cream and drizzle with chocolate sauce, if using, or maple syrup. Serve with coconut flakes and sliced bananas, if you're feeling fancy.

ELECTRIC GRIDDLE OR LARGE NONSTICK SKILLET

1-1/4 cups unbleached all-purpose flour 300 mL

1 tbsp lightly packed brown sugar 15 mL

2 tbsp baking powder 30 mL

1/4 tsp salt 1 mL

1/2 cup unsweetened soy or almond milk 125 mL

1/2 cup Baileys Almande 125 mL

1 tsp vanilla extract 5 mL

1/4 cup peanut butter 60 mL

1 tbsp coconut oil 15 mL

Chantilly Cream (page 252), optional

Chocolate Sauce (page 264), optional

Pure maple syrup

Coconut flakes (optional)

Banana slices (optional)

Peanut Butter and Jam French Toast

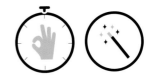

SERVES 4

Hi. I'm Candice, and I'm a sugar addict. (*Hiiii, Caaaandice.*) Maybe I subconsciously crave sweets for breakfast because my mother wouldn't let us eat sugary cereal, and I'm making up for lost time. Or maybe it's the three mimosas I have before I start cooking on a Sunday. Either way, this indulgent pocket of PB&J love is the French toast of my dreams.

1. In a blender, combine melted vegan butter, almond milk, coconut sugar, tofu, nutritional yeast and vanilla. Blend on High until smooth and creamy. Transfer to a large bowl.

2. Spread 1 tbsp (15 mL) peanut butter on a slice of bread and 1 tbsp (15 mL) raspberry jam on another slice of bread and smush them together. Congrats, you've just made a peanut butter & jam sandwich. Repeat with remaining bread and PB&J.

3. In a large skillet, melt vegan butter over medium-high heat. Dip one PB&J sandwich in tofu mixture and coat both sides generously.

4. Place sandwich in the pan and cook for 3 to 4 minutes, until golden brown. Flip and cook for about 3 to 4 minutes, until golden. Remove from pan and repeat with the remaining sandwiches and tofu mixture, adjusting heat and buttering pan between batches, as necessary.

5. Serve hot, topped with maple syrup and confectioners' sugar or Raspberry Coulis (page 254), and a side of veggie sausage (Hack It! page 41) and Ginger Kombucha Mimosas (page 244)!

BLENDER
CAST-IRON OR
NONSTICK SKILLET

2 tbsp melted vegan butter 30 mL

1/2 cup unsweetened almond milk 125 mL

2 tbsp coconut sugar 30 mL

3-1/2 oz soft silken tofu 100 g

2 tbsp nutritional yeast 30 mL

1 tsp vanilla extract 5 mL

1/4 cup peanut butter 60 mL

8 slices sourdough bread (about 1 loaf) 8

1/4 cup raspberry jam 60 mL

1 tbsp vegan butter (approx.) 15 mL

Pure maple syrup

Organic confectioners' (icing) sugar

HACK IT!

When frying, I like to cook the outside edges of the sandwich by standing it upright until crispy, about 2 minutes per side.

Try this French toast with any nut butter or spread that you love. Vegan chocolate hazelnut spread is divine.

Loaded Breakfast Burritos

MAKES 2 LARGE BURRITOS

We live for Tex-Mex and brunch. Mash up the two and you have the ultimate meal. We've been devouring these breakfast burritos every weekend since our trip to Nicaragua three years ago, where — yup, you guessed it — we ate breakfast burritos every day.

1. **Hash and Beans:** In a medium bowl, combine sweet potato, 1/2 tsp (2 mL) cumin, 1/4 tsp (1 mL) sea salt, pepper to taste and olive oil; toss to coat.

2. Spread sweet potato on a prepared baking sheet. Roast in preheated oven for about 20 minutes, flipping halfway through, until tender. Remove from oven and set aside.

3. Meanwhile, in a medium skillet, heat coconut oil over medium heat. Add garlic and sauté for about 2 minutes, until fragrant. Add remaining cumin and chili powder; sauté for about 1 minute, until fragrant. Add pinto beans and cook, stirring occasionally, for about 5 minutes, until heated through. Sprinkle with remaining sea salt and remove from heat. Using a potato masher or a fork, mash bean mixture to desired texture. Some people like it really smooth, but I prefer to leave some whole beans in there for texture. Cover and set aside.

4. **Burritos:** Heat a large, dry skillet over medium heat. Place 1 tortilla in skillet and heat for about 30 seconds to 1 minute on each side, until warm and pliable. Transfer to a plate. Spread roughly 1/4 cup (50 mL) refried beans along the length of the center of tortilla. Top with half the tofu scramble, sweet potato, salsa and avocado slices and a sprinkling of jalapeño and cilantro. Add more beans if your tortilla allows, or save for another recipe.

5. Roll tortilla burrito-style, place back into hot, dry skillet over medium heat and toast both sides and the ends. This will help your burrito stay together. Now, do it all again with the other burrito. Twinsies!

PREHEAT OVEN TO 400°F (200°C)

BAKING SHEET LINED WITH PARCHMENT PAPER

HASH AND BEANS

1 medium sweet potato, peeled and diced small 1

1-1/2 tsp ground cumin, divided 7 mL

3/4 tsp sea salt, divided 3 mL

Freshly ground black pepper

1 tbsp olive oil 15 mL

1-1/2 tsp coconut oil 7 mL

2 garlic cloves, minced

1/4 tsp chili powder 1 mL

1 can (14 oz/398 mL) pinto beans, with liquid 1

BURRITOS

2 large flour tortillas 2

1 recipe Better Than Eggs: Tofu Scramble (page 36) 1

1/2 cup Austin-Tacious Roasted Salsa (page 150) 125 mL

1 avocado, thinly sliced 1

1 jalapeño pepper, seeded and finely chopped 1

1/4 cup finely chopped fresh cilantro 60 mL

~ HACK IT! ~

Love to dip? Whip up some Burrito-Worthy Sour Cream (page 51) or The Art of Cheese Sauce (page 52), serve along with a side of your favorite hot sauce and dip away!

Veggs Benny

SERVES 4

Brunch is a very important part of our weekend-warrior ritual, but it can be difficult to accommodate the needs of an omni/vegan party of two. Since a brunchless life is not an option, one afternoon we decided to create the "at home" version of Eggs Benny. It has become a household ritual so beloved that it's practically a religion.

1. In a large bowl, combine asparagus and olive oil; toss to coat. Arrange in a single layer on a prepared baking sheet, and roast in preheated oven for 10 to 15 minutes, until tender but still crisp.

2. While your asparagus is roasting, heat coconut oil in a large skillet over medium-high heat. When oil begins to shimmer, add tofu and a pinch of salt and pepper. (Don't be shy with the salt: tofu literally has no flavor, so salt with conviction!) Cook for 10 minutes on each side, flipping once, until tofu starts to brown on the edges, just like an egg would. Set aside.

3. Heat the same pan you used to prepare the tofu over medium-high heat. Lightly fry cold cuts for about 3 minutes, flipping once, until heated and slightly crispy. Congratulations, you've just made vegan bacon!

4. Place 2 English muffin pieces on each plate and top first with cold-cut bacon slices, then tofu egg, followed by asparagus spears. Drizzle with hollandaise sauce and add a sprinkle of cayenne and chopped chives. Serve immediately and say "So long" to that hangover!

> PREHEAT OVEN TO 400°F (200°C)
> BAKING SHEET LINED WITH PARCHMENT PAPER

12 asparagus spears, trimmed 12
1/2 tsp olive oil 2 mL
1 tbsp coconut oil 15 mL
1 block (10 oz/300 g) medium or soft tofu, cut into 8 slices, about 1/2 inch (1 cm) thick 1
Salt and freshly ground black pepper
8 slices of your favorite vegan cold cuts (I like Tofurky), sliced into bacon-like strips 8
4 English muffins, halved 4
1 recipe Ritzy Hollandaise (page 53) 1
Cayenne pepper
Chopped chives

~~ HACK IT! ~~

We love this dish with asparagus, but if it isn't your thing, you can totally leave it out.

When asparagus is not in season, try this recipe with a handful of steamed spinach or kale instead or even our fabulous lox (page 81).

Get creative: use leftover Better Than Eggs: Tofu Scramble (page 36) or any aging vegetables you have lying around for an easy repurposed dish.

The All-Day Breakfast Sandwich

SERVES 4

Fun fact: we live above a McDonald's. While it's been easy to keep James out of there *most* of the time, wrestling with him on a Saturday morning before 11 a.m. has become a creative feat. This sandwich is so easy it could practically make itself. I have it ready and waiting before he can even plan his escape.

1. Stand the block of tofu on its side and slice in half lengthwise. Then cut each half crosswise. You should have four equal-size squares.

2. In a medium skillet, heat coconut oil over medium heat. Place tofu squares in the skillet; sprinkle with black salt and pepper. Fry tofu for about 4 minutes, until lightly browned. Flip, season with additional salt and pepper, and fry for an additional 4 minutes, or until the edges of tofu are slightly browned and heated through. Remove from heat.

3. Meanwhile, toast English muffins and smear with vegan cheese sauce. (If you are using vegan cheese slices, place one slice of cheese on each tofu square, and cover skillet with a lid. Warm on low heat for roughly 2 minutes, until cheese becomes soft.)

4. Arrange 2 slices of bacon on one half of an English muffin. Place one square of tofu on top and add 1 to 2 slices of avocado. Give it a squirt of Sriracha sauce and place a muffin half on top. Repeat with remaining ingredients and say, "I'm vegan' it."

1 package (7 oz/210 g) smoked tofu 1
1 tbsp coconut oil 15 mL
Black salt or sea salt
Freshly ground black pepper
4 English muffins, halved 4
4 tbsp The Art of Cheese Sauce (page 52) or 4 store-bought vegan Cheddar cheese slices 60 mL
8 slices vegan bacon of choice (pages 45 to 48) 8
1/2 avocado, sliced 1/2
Sriracha sauce

~~~ HACK IT! ~~~

Try this with hollandaise sauce (page 53) instead of cheese.

For an extra-spicy kick, try adding a layer of pickled jalapeño.

Southern Biscuits and Gravy

SERVES 4

Only Southern folks could convince the world that gravy is okay for breakfast. I'm all about these flaky biscuits smothered in creamy country gravy, and I'm not about to apologize for it. #SorryNotSorry

1. **Country Gravy:** In a deep, heavy-bottomed saucepan, melt vegan butter over medium heat. Add flour, garlic powder, 1/2 tsp (2 mL) sea salt and 1/2 tsp (2 mL) pepper; cook, whisking constantly, for about 10 minutes, until browned and smooth. Do not burn.

2. Very slowly, whisk in soy milk and cook, stirring constantly, for about 5 minutes, to avoid lumping and burning. Add bouillon cube and cook, whisking, for about 10 minutes, until bubbling and thickened. If the gravy becomes too thick, add a little more soy milk. Taste as you go and season with sea salt and pepper. Add vegan bacon, if using. Remove from heat and cover with a lid to keep warm. Reheat slightly, if necessary, to serve.

3. **Buttermilk Biscuits:** In a small bowl, combine soy milk and apple cider vinegar to make vegan buttermilk. Place in fridge for 10 minutes.

4. In a stand mixer or a large bowl, combine flour, baking powder, baking soda, sea salt and sugar. Mix until well combined. Add vegan butter, 1 tbsp (15 mL) at a time, mixing until the dough looks like pea-shaped sand. If you are doing this by hand, use a pastry blender or fork. Work quickly so the butter doesn't get too warm. In your stand mixer, you can do this at Stir speed, mixing for 1 minute.

5. Add buttermilk mixture, 1/4 cup (60 mL) at a time, and mix until dough begins to form. AVOID OVERBEATING. If you are doing this by hand, use a fork.

6. On a floured surface, turn dough over on itself and lightly dust with flour. Do this about 6 times. DO NOT OVERKNEAD. Form dough into a 1-inch (2.5 cm) thick long oval. Using a round cutter or glass, cut dough into large rounds.

7. Place biscuits on a prepared baking sheet, just touching one another. Collect all dough scraps and cut until you run out of dough. Brush the tops with melted butter, and bake in the preheated oven for 10 to 12 minutes, until golden. Serve warm with country gravy.

PREHEAT OVEN TO 450°F (230°C)
DEEP, HEAVY-BOTTOMED SAUCEPAN
BAKING SHEET LINED WITH PARCHMENT PAPER
STAND MIXER OR PASTRY BLENDER (OPTIONAL)
2-1/2-INCH (6 CM) ROUND CUTTER (OPTIONAL)

COUNTRY GRAVY

1/4 cup vegan butter 60 mL
1/3 cup unbleached all-purpose flour 75 mL
1 tsp garlic powder 5 mL
Sea salt and freshly ground black pepper
2 cups unsweetened soy milk (approx.) 500 mL
1 vegetarian bouillon cube 1
Vegan bacon of choice (pages 45 to 48) or vegan sausage (Hack It! page 41), optional

BUTTERMILK BISCUITS

3/4 cup unsweetened soy milk, cold 175 mL
1 tsp apple cider vinegar 5 mL
3 cups unbleached all-purpose white flour 750 mL
2-1/2 tsp baking powder 12 mL
1 tsp baking soda 5 mL
1/2 tsp sea salt 2 mL
1 tsp sugar 5 mL
1/2 cup vegan butter, cold, cut into cubes 125 mL
Unbleached all-purpose flour for dusting
Melted vegan butter for brushing

HACK IT!

Flour tastes just like . . . flour, so make sure it's cooked. If you taste flour in your gravy, it didn't cook for long enough. When you're making gravy, really make sure to taste it every couple of minutes to ensure that the flour taste is gone.

Make sure your butter is cold, fool! You will not get fluffy biscuits with room-temperature butter.

Leftover gravy can be stored in the fridge for 5 to 7 days. The biscuits, however, should be consumed within 2 days. To reheat the gravy, whisk in a saucepan over medium-low heat for about 5 to 8 minutes, until heated through.

Chive and Sriracha Beer Waffles

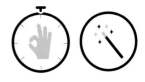

SERVES 2

Ever heard the saying "You can make anything better with Sriracha sauce"? Maybe not, but it's true. I also think that everything's better with beer. So, these waffles are perfect for those mornings when you wake up really craving a cold one, but it's 9 a.m., and that's socially unacceptable. Cheers!

1. **Maple Sriracha Sauce:** In a small bowl, whisk together sour cream, Sriracha sauce, maple syrup and salt. Transfer to a squeeze bottle, mason jar or container and place in the fridge.

2. **Savory Waffles:** In a large bowl, whisk together flour, thyme, chives, salt, baking powder, baking soda and sugar.

3. In a stand mixer, beat aquafaba on High for 10 to 15 minutes, until soft peaks form.

4. Slowly add beer and melted vegan butter to flour mixture, whisking until smooth. Fold in whipped aquafaba. Let stand while you preheat your waffle iron.

5. Grease a waffle iron, and ladle batter, 1/4 cup (60 mL) at a time, until the surface is almost completely covered (about 1 cup/250 mL total, or use the amount that fits in your waffle maker). Cook for about 7 to 10 minutes or according to waffle-maker instructions, until golden brown. Remove cooked waffle from the iron, transfer to a baking sheet and keep warm in the preheated oven. Cook waffles until you run out of batter, greasing lightly in between batches. Serve waffles with a drizzle of maple Sriracha sauce, additional Sriracha sauce, if desired, and green onions.

~~ HACK IT! ~~

Aquafaba is the liquid found in a can of chickpeas, and it makes a wonderful replacement for eggs. Don't be discouraged if you don't get perfect peaks while beating the aquafaba. It will still hold the waffles together.

Try this with our Famous Edgy Veg Fried Chicken (page 174) and maple syrup for an indulgent chicken-and-waffles breakfast. Yummy!

PREHEAT OVEN TO 200°F
(100°C)
STAND MIXER WITH THE
WHISK ATTACHMENT OR
HAND MIXER
WAFFLE IRON

MAPLE SRIRACHA SAUCE
1/2 cup Burrito-Worthy Sour Cream (page 51) 125 mL
1 tbsp Sriracha sauce 15 mL
2 tbsp pure maple syrup 30 mL
1/2 tsp salt 2 mL

SAVORY WAFFLES
3 cups unbleached all-purpose flour 750 mL
2 tbsp chopped fresh thyme 30 mL
2 tbsp chopped fresh chives 30 mL
1 tsp salt 5 mL
2 tbsp baking powder 30 mL
2 tsp baking soda 10 mL
2 tsp organic sugar 10 mL
2/3 cup aquafaba 150 mL
3 cups dark or amber beer 750 mL
1/2 cup vegan butter, melted 125 mL
Vegetable or coconut oil
Sriracha sauce (optional)
3 green onions, white and light green parts only, thinly sliced 3

Shakshuka, Habibi!

SERVES 4

Although the Middle East can't agree on much, shakshuka has managed to cross all borders, and it's easy to see why. This one-skillet meal is quick, healthy, easy to scale up or down and works for breakfast, brunch, lunch or dinner.

1. **Shakshuka:** In a blender, combine tofu, nutritional yeast and black salt; blend on High until smooth. Set aside.

2. In a large skillet, heat 2 tbsp (30 mL) coconut oil over medium heat. Add onion, red pepper, jalapeño and garlic; sauté for about 5 minutes, until soft. Add cumin and paprika; cook, stirring constantly, for about 1 minute, until fragrant. Stirring constantly, add tomato paste and cook for 1 minute, until fragrant and bubbling slightly. Add tomatoes, bay leaf, 1/2 tsp (2 mL) sea salt and 1/4 tsp (1 mL) pepper; stir and bring to a boil. Immediately reduce heat to medium-low, cover and simmer, stirring occasionally, for about 10 minutes, until sauce has thickened. Add more sea salt and pepper to taste.

3. Heat 1 tbsp (15 mL) coconut oil in a medium skillet over medium-high heat. Add tofu mixture and cook, stirring occasionally, for about 10 minutes, until thick and the liquid has evaporated. Set aside.

4. Using a wooden spoon, evenly space four wells in the sauce. Evenly divide tofu mixture between each well. Cover and simmer for about 5 minutes, until edges of tofu are slightly orange from the sauce. Transfer to the preheated oven and bake, uncovered, for about 10 minutes, until tops of tofu eggs are just set.

5. Pull the shakshuka out of the oven, fan out avocado slices in the center and sprinkle with parsley. Serve with a side of warm bread. It is customary in our home to scoop up the remaining sauce with a piece of bread, so go ahead and eat with your hands!

HACK IT!

Try this with some greens like spinach or chopped kale, mixed into the sauce in Step 2.

PREHEAT OVEN TO 400°F (200°C)
BLENDER
LARGE, OVEN-SAFE CAST-IRON SKILLET WITH LID

SHAKSHUKA
2 packages (each 14 oz/400 g) soft tofu 2
1/4 cup nutritional yeast 60 mL
1/2 tsp black salt or sea salt 2 mL
3 tbsp coconut oil, divided 45 mL
1 onion, chopped 1
1 large red bell pepper, diced 1
1 jalapeño pepper, seeded and minced 1
4 garlic cloves, minced 4
1 tsp ground cumin 5 mL
1 tbsp sweet Hungarian paprika 15 mL
1/4 cup tomato paste 60 mL
1 can (28 oz /796 mL) crushed tomatoes 1
1 bay leaf 1
Sea salt and freshly ground black pepper

ACCOUTREMENTS
1/2 avocado, sliced 1/2
1/4 cup curly parsley, roughly chopped 60 mL
Warm crusty white bread or Lebanese-style pita (optional)

UnOrthodox Lox and Cream Cheese Bagels

SERVES 2

Growing up, James ate lox on cream cheese almost every weekend. Purchasing freshly baked bagels with all the fixings was a family ritual. How on earth was I supposed to recreate the taste and texture of cured salmon? As with every recipe I create, I researched the traditional method and adapted it. Carrots may be unorthodox, but James says they're better than the real thing. #winning

1. Pour a layer of sea salt into a baking dish to completely cover the bottom. Brush each sheet of nori with a tiny bit of water and wrap around each carrot. Arrange wrapped carrots in the baking dish side by side and completely cover with remaining sea salt. Bake in preheated oven for 1-1/2 hours.

2. Place the baking dish on a wire rack and let cool for about 30 minutes, until you can handle the carrots. Using a spoon or fork, carefully move salt away from carrots and carefully unwrap carrots, discarding nori. Peel off the skin from each carrot. (It's okay if you don't get all the skin off.)

3. Using a very sharp knife, slice carrots lengthwise, alternating between thin strips and sashimi-style sushi pieces. Place in a medium glass container or bowl.

4. In a small bowl, whisk together water, apple cider vinegar, rice vinegar, miso paste, soy sauce, liquid smoke, kelp and lemon juice. Add flaxseed oil and continue to whisk. Pour over carrots and gently mix to saturate each piece. Cover and refrigerate for at least 24 hours, but preferably 48 hours. Gently mix about twice a day. If carrots start to look dry, add 1 tbsp (15 mL) flaxseed oil and mix to combine.

5. Remove carrot lox from the fridge and let come to room temperature.

6. Slice bagels through the center and toast until golden brown.

7. Smear each bagel half with vegan cream cheese and top with carrot lox. Add a thin layer of red onion slices and sprinkle with capers, dill and chives. Season with sea salt and pepper to taste. Serve with 1 lemon wedge per bagel and squeeze juice over both halves.

PREHEAT OVEN TO 400°F (200°C)
9-INCH (23 CM) SQUARE GLASS BAKING DISH

- **2 cups** coarse sea salt 500 mL
- **4 8-inch** (20 cm) nori sheets, cut in half lengthwise 4
- **Water for** brushing
- **8 large** carrots (unpeeled) 8
- **1/2 cup** water 125 mL
- **2 tbsp** apple cider vinegar 30 mL
- **2 tbsp** seasoned rice vinegar 30 mL
- **1 tbsp** white miso paste 15 mL
- **2 tbsp** soy sauce or tamari 30 mL
- **1 tsp** liquid smoke 5 mL
- **2 tbsp** kelp granules 30 mL
- **1 tsp** freshly squeezed lemon juice 5 mL
- **3 tbsp** flaxseed oil (approx.) 45 mL
- **4 bagels** 4
- **2 cups** vegan cream cheese 500 mL
- **Red onion,** thinly sliced
- **2 tbsp** capers, drained 30 mL
- **1/4 cup** roughly chopped fresh dill 60 mL
- **1/4 cup** roughly chopped fresh chives 60 mL
- **Sea salt** and freshly ground black pepper
- **4 lemon** wedges 4

Souper Natural

/'so̅o̅pər 'naCH(ə)rəl/ *adjective*

1. (Of a substance or dish resembling soup) exquisitely pleasing in a way that defies scientific understanding or the laws of nature • *"Hey, Ruth, this pho is so good, it's souper natural!"*

SOUP GETS A BAD RAP. It doesn't have to be boring and come from a can on days when your boyfriend is home sick from work. This delicious group of brews will warm your heart and stomach on the coldest of days, and they will keep your guests wondering what magical plant-based powers you've cast into your cauldron.

What the Pho

SERVES 4

I really love pho. So I created this recipe just pho me. The rich and flavorful mushroom broth is pho-nomenal, and the noodles and fresh veggies are so pho-king delicious. If I could, I would eat this pho-ever. I suggest you try it; soup is good pho the soul.

1. **Broth:** Arrange onions and ginger in a single layer on a baking sheet. Place the baking sheet directly under the broiler; broil for 5 minutes on each side, until the onions and ginger pieces are charred slightly. Transfer to a colander and rinse with cold water.

2. In a large stock pot, combine cinnamon, star anise, cloves and coriander. Dry-roast over medium-low heat, stirring constantly, for 1 to 2 minutes, until fragrant. DO NOT BURN. Add onions, ginger, sesame oil, vinegar, garlic, 8 cups (2 L) water, bouillon cubes, mushrooms, soy sauce, mirin and carrots. Bring to a boil over medium-high heat. Immediately reduce heat, cover and simmer over low heat for 1 to 5 hours. (If I have the time, I simmer for a full 5 hours, but let's be serious, I'm busy, and 1 to 2 hours is about all my patience can handle.)

3. Bring a large saucepan of salted water to a boil. Add bok choy and rice noodles; cook according to rice noodle package instructions (typically 1 to 3 minutes, depending on width of noodles). Using a slotted spoon, remove bok choy once it is bright green and place in a small bowl. Drain noodles and run them under cool water. Immediately divide noodles between the serving bowls.

4. **Toppings:** Place Sriracha sauce and hoisin sauce in two separate small bowls. Arrange bok choy, mushrooms, green onions, red Thai chiles, lime, bean sprouts, cilantro, basil, mint and the bowls of sauces on a serving dish or platter.

5. Strain broth over a fine-mesh sieve into a large bowl, discarding solids. Season to taste with sea salt. Ladle broth over noodle bowls and top each with a quarter of the seitan. Serve with toppings, and let guests top their soup as they wish.

HACK IT!

Try this with our seitan chicken (page 38) or fried smoked tofu for a quick and easy flavor swap.

PREHEAT BROILER
FINE-MESH SIEVE

BROTH
2 medium white onions, quartered 2
1 4-inch (10 cm) piece fresh ginger, quartered 1
2 cinnamon sticks 2
2 star anise pods 2
3 whole cloves 3
2 tsp coriander seeds 10 mL
1 tsp toasted sesame oil 5 mL
1 tbsp seasoned rice vinegar 15 mL
4 garlic cloves, crushed 4
Water
4 vegetable bouillon cubes 4
1 cup sliced cremini mushrooms 250 mL
1/4 cup soy sauce or tamari 60 mL
1 tbsp mirin 15 mL
2 carrots, roughly chopped 2
8 baby bok choy, halved 8
14 oz dried rice noodles 400 g

TOPPINGS
Sriracha sauce
Hoisin sauce
1/2 cup sliced shiitake mushroom caps 125 mL
4 green onions, thinly sliced 4
2 red Thai chiles, sliced 2
1 lime, cut into wedges 1
1 cup bean sprouts 250 mL
1/4 cup fresh cilantro 60 mL
1/4 cup fresh basil 60 mL
1/4 cup fresh mint 60 mL
Sea salt
1 cup sliced Seitan Mastery 2.0: Beef (page 40) 250 mL

Momofuku-Style Ramen

SERVES 2

I have an obsession with David Chang and his career as a chef. I'm beyond fan-girl status, and the countless hours I've spent binge-watching him on Netflix are to blame for the obscene amount of time I've spent perfecting ramen broth. When I was testing this recipe, we literally ate nothing but ramen for a week, until it was perfect! Even David Chang (*I love you*) would approve.

1. **Broth:** In a large stock pot, bring water to a boil over high heat. Remove from heat, add kombu and let steep for 1 hour.

2. While the kombu is steeping, in a medium saucepan, heat 1 tbsp (15 mL) sesame oil over medium-high heat. Add onion, garlic and sea salt; sauté for about 5 minutes, until onion is translucent and soft. Add carrots, cremini mushrooms, ginger and sesame seeds; sauté for 10 minutes, until mushrooms are soft.

3. Once the kombu has steeped, remove it with tongs and discard.

4. Add onion mixture to stock pot and bring to a gentle simmer over medium heat; cook for 15 minutes, stirring occasionally. Using a slotted spoon, skim off any foamy particles that rise to the top. Add remaining 1 tbsp (15 mL) sesame oil, ground shiitake mushrooms, pepper, chile bean paste, chile oil, tamari, bouillon cubes, vegan Worcestershire, agave and nutritional yeast; cover, leaving some space for steam to escape, and reduce heat to low. Simmer for 2 hours, skimming the top with a slotted spoon occasionally, or until broth has reduced by roughly one-quarter. Strain through a fine-mesh sieve into a second stock pot or large bowl, discarding solids.

5. Heat broth on low heat. Add mirin, if using, and 5 tbsp (75 mL) miso paste; stir until well combined. Taste and season broth with an additional 1 tbsp (15 mL) miso, sea salt and chile oil, if desired. Add seitan slices. Increase heat to medium and simmer for about 5 minutes, until slices are heated through. Using a slotted spoon, remove seitan, set aside in a bowl and cover to keep warm. Reduce heat of broth to low and keep warm until needed.

6. Meanwhile, bring a large pot of water to a boil. Add noodles and cook for 2 to 2-1/2 minutes, until tender. Drain and divide between four bowls. Divide broth between bowls and arrange bean sprouts, green onions, nori, corn, enoki mushrooms and seitan beef overtop. Serve with additional chile oil and sesame oil for guests to drizzle on top to taste.

FINE-MESH SIEVE

BROTH
16 cups water 4 L
2 oz kombu 60 g
2 tbsp toasted sesame oil, divided 30 mL
2 cups roughly chopped onion 500 mL
3 garlic cloves, crushed 3
1/2 tsp sea salt 2 mL
1-1/2 cups chopped carrots 375 mL
3 cups chopped cremini mushrooms 750 mL
1 1-inch (2.5 cm) piece fresh ginger, sliced 1
1 tbsp sesame seeds 15 mL
1 oz dried shiitake mushrooms, ground 30 g
1/2 tsp freshly ground black pepper 2 mL
1 tbsp chile bean paste 15 mL
1 tbsp Asian chile oil 15 mL
1/4 cup tamari 60 mL
2 vegan beef bouillon cubes 2
3 tbsp vegan Worcestershire 45 mL
1 tbsp agave nectar 15 mL
2 tbsp nutritional yeast 30 mL
2 tbsp mirin (optional) 30 mL
6 tbsp white miso paste 90 mL
2 cups sliced Seitan Mastery 2.0: Beef (page 40) 500 mL
4 packages (each 5 oz/150 g) dried ramen noodles 4

TOPPINGS (page 87)

HACK IT!

I understand that you're probably scratching your head on where to find dried and ground shiitake mushrooms. Well, we make them ourselves. Dried shiitake mushrooms are available at most grocery stores, so just grind them up in a high-powered blender, food processor or my personal favorite, a coffee (or spice) grinder.

You can find most of these ingredients at any Asian grocery store (where I spend most of my time) or in the international section of a really good supermarket.

This broth is best made 2 to 3 days prior to use. It really lets the flavors mingle. After Step 4, store prepared broth in a container and keep for up to 7 days in the fridge or 3 months in the freezer. Reheat and finish Steps 5 and 6.

TOPPINGS

2 cups bean sprouts 500 mL
4 green onions, thinly sliced 4
2 nori sheets, quartered 2
1 cup drained canned corn
    kernels 250 mL
2 cups enoki mushrooms
    500 mL
Asian chile oil
Toasted sesame oil

Superbowl Chili

SERVES 4 TO 6

If only I could bottle up a male sports fan's enthusiasm and use it when *I* need something done — like the dishes or putting down the toilet seat. Ladies, whenever your jersey-clad dude starts yelling, "Baby, baby, look!" as though he's mistaken you for someone who actually cares about whatever game is on, just give him bowl of this stuff, sit back and smell the silence . . .

1. In a large stock pot, heat olive oil over medium-high heat. Add onion and garlic; sauté for about 3 to 5 minutes, until translucent. Add cumin, basil, oregano, cayenne and red pepper flakes; sauté for about 1 minute, until fragrant. Add texturized vegetable protein, tomato paste and mushrooms; sauté for about 5 minutes, until mushrooms are tender.

2. Add tomatoes, beer, espresso, kidney beans, black beans and maple syrup; bring to a boil. Immediately reduce heat and add 1/2 tsp (2 mL) each sea salt and pepper. Cover and simmer for 1 hour, stirring occasionally, until flavors are rich and chili has thickened slightly.

3. Season to taste with sea salt and pepper. Garnish with a dollop of sour cream, Cheddar cheese and parsley, if desired. Serve with a smile and a tallboy.

HACK IT!

Cornbread is ideal for collecting any leftover chili clinging to your bowl. It's kind of like licking your plate, but socially acceptable.

Chili gets better with age (as most soups and stews do). This is even better a day or two after you make it. After Step 2, store in a container and keep in the fridge for up to 7 days and in the freezer for 3 months, then reheat until bubbling and continue with Step 3.

2 tbsp olive oil 30 mL
1 medium onion, diced 1
4 garlic cloves, minced 4
1 tbsp ground cumin 15 mL
1 tsp dried basil 5 mL
1 tsp dried oregano 5 mL
1 tsp cayenne pepper 5 mL
1 tsp red pepper flakes 5 mL
1 cup textured vegetable protein or veggie ground round 250 mL
1 can (5-1/2 oz/156 mL) tomato paste 1
1 cup sliced cremini mushrooms 250 mL
1 can (28 oz/796 mL) diced tomatoes, with juices 1
1 can or bottle (12 oz/341 mL) dark beer 1
1/4 cup brewed espresso 60 mL
2 cups canned or cooked kidney beans, drained and rinsed 500 mL
2 cups canned or cooked black beans, drained and rinsed 500 mL
1/2 cup pure maple syrup 125 mL
Sea salt and freshly ground black pepper
Burrito-Worthy Sour Cream (page 51), optional
Vegan Cheddar cheese shreds, optional
Fresh flat-leaf (Italian) parsley, optional

Tomato Bisque and Grilled Cheese

SERVES 4

James first discovered the comfort of a tomato bisque paired with grilled cheese while living far from home, in Washington. It became the inspiration for this rich, creamy tomato bisque and cheesy, crunchy, buttery grilled cheese. Make this whenever you're in need of a quick and easy dinner or a warm hug when you're far away from home. Pairs well with a crisp, white wine.

1. **Tomato Bisque:** In a medium saucepan, heat vegan butter over medium heat. Add garlic and sauté for 1 minute, until fragrant. Stir in tomato paste and cook for 1 minute, until fragrant. Add tomatoes, cayenne, basil, thyme and onion powder; cook, stirring constantly, for 5 minutes, until well combined and fragrant.

2. Add bouillon cubes, water, maple syrup, bay leaf and sea salt; bring to a boil. Immediately reduce heat to medium-low and simmer for 10 minutes, until bouillon cubes have dissolved.

3. Transfer soup to a blender, reserving one-quarter of mixture in the pot. Remove the plug in the lid and blend on High, until smooth. Return to the saucepan and simmer on medium-low for 20 minutes.

4. Stir in cream and keep warm over low heat while preparing grilled cheese. Taste and add more sea salt and pepper, if desired.

5. **Grilled Cheese:** Meanwhile, make grilled cheese sandwiches. Spread 1-1/2 tsp (7 mL) vegan butter on one side of each bread slice.

6. Heat a large skillet over medium-low heat. (The key to perfect grilled cheese is cooking it low and slow). Working in batches as necessary, place bread slices, butter side down, in the skillet. Top each with 2 to 3 tbsp (30 to 45 mL) cheese sauce or 2 cheese slices and a second slice of bread, butter side up. Cook for about 4 minutes, until bottom slice turns a nice golden brown. Flip sandwiches and cover the skillet with a lid to help melt cheese. Toast for about 4 minutes, until the second side is golden brown and cheese is melted. Keep an eye on it, because it can burn.

BLENDER

TOMATO BISQUE

1/4 cup vegan butter 60 mL
2 garlic cloves, minced 2
1/2 cup + 2 tbsp tomato paste 155 mL
4 plum (Roma) tomatoes, finely diced 4
1/8 tsp cayenne pepper 0.5 mL
1/2 tsp dried basil 2 mL
1/2 tsp dried thyme 2 mL
1 tsp onion powder 5 mL
2 vegetable bouillon cubes 2
4 cups water 1 L
1 tbsp pure maple syrup 15 mL
1 bay leaf 1
1/2 tsp sea salt (approx.) 2 mL
1 cup Essential Non-Dairy Cream (page 49) 250 mL
1/4 tsp freshly ground black pepper (approx.) 1 mL

GRILLED CHEESE

8 slices (1/2-inch/1 cm thick) bread 8
1/4 cup vegan butter, softened, divided 60 mL
1 cup The Art of Cheese Sauce (page 52) or 8 slices store-bought American-style cheese slices 250 mL
1/4 cup fresh flat-leaf (Italian) parsley, finely chopped 60 mL

7. Ladle soup into bowls, sprinkle with chopped parsley and serve with grilled cheese sandwiches to dip.

HACK IT!

For the ultimate crispiness, spread vegan mayo on the bread instead of vegan butter and add 1-1/2 tsp (7 mL) butter to the skillet while toasting. This will provide a crispier, golden toast.

Spread pesto on the bread instead of vegan butter for a flavor twist, or add minced garlic to the butter before spreading to make garlic grilled cheese.

#SweaterWeather Pumpkin Sage Soup

SERVES 4 TO 6

I'm lazy AF in the winter. As soon as October hits, I head straight into a six-month hibernation. I don't shave my legs and avoid going outside, and cooking becomes a serious chore. During SAD season, I like to hack dinner and spend one afternoon making soup that I can freeze. For all you fellow bears out there, this recipe is a great place to start.

1. In a large stock pot, heat coconut oil over medium-high heat. Add onion and garlic; sauté for about 3 to 5 minutes, until translucent. Add coriander, chili powder, sage, celery, carrots and potato; sauté for 5 minutes, until the potato starts to stick to the pot.

2. Add bouillon cubes, water, pumpkin, lemon juice, 2 tsp (10 mL) sea salt and 1 tsp (5 mL) pepper; stir to combine. Bring to a boil; immediately reduce heat to medium-low and simmer for 40 minutes, stirring occasionally, until thickened slightly.

3. In three batches, carefully transfer soup to blender. Remove the plug in the lid and blend on High, until completely smooth. Transfer back to the stock pot, warm over medium heat and season to taste with sea salt and pepper. Garnish with fresh sage leaves, if desired.

HIGH-POWERED BLENDER

2 tbsp coconut oil 30 mL
1 large white onion, sliced 1
4 garlic cloves, minced 4
2 tsp coriander seeds 10 mL
1 tsp chili powder 5 mL
2 tbsp dried sage 30 mL
1 celery stalk, chopped 1
2 carrots, chopped 2
1 yellow-flesh potato, peeled and diced 1
2 vegetable bouillon cubes 2
4 cups water 1 L
6 cups pumpkin purée (fresh or canned) 1.5 L
1 tbsp freshly squeezed lemon juice 15 mL
Sea salt and freshly ground black pepper
Fresh sage leaves (optional)

 ## HACK IT!

If you're a spice freak like I am, drizzle some spicy chile oil over the top before serving, then sprinkle with red pepper flakes.

To make pumpkin purée: Preheat oven to 400°F (200°C). Cut a large pumpkin in half and place cut side down on a baking sheet lined with parchment paper. Roast for about 45 minutes, until skin is dark and flesh is soft. Remove from the oven, let cool for 15 minutes and scoop flesh from skin with a spoon. Transfer to a food processor and purée until smooth.

Très Flawless French Onion Soup

SERVES 4

I may have #WokeUpLikeThis, but this soup sure as heck didn't make itself. Like the making of a #1 Beyoncé song, each element of this fierce French onion soup was meticulously crafted. Pass me a vat, I'm about to get drunk in love on this stuff. #bowdown

1. In a large stock pot, bring water and sea salt to a boil over high heat. Immediately reduce heat to a simmer; add porcini mushrooms, oyster mushrooms, shiitake mushrooms, carrots, celery, soy sauce, vegan Worcestershire, nutritional yeast, bay leaves, thyme, peppercorns and garlic. Cover and simmer for 1-1/2 hours, until broth is slightly reduced. Make sure to taste along the way. It should start to taste rich and full of flavor. Add 1 tsp (5 mL) sea salt, if necessary.

2. Strain through a fine-mesh sieve into a second stock pot or large bowl, discarding solids. Now you have a beef-style broth. Set aside.

3. Preheat oven to 325°F (160°C).

4. Heat the stock pot that was used to cook the mushrooms over medium-low heat. Add 1 tbsp (15 mL) olive oil and vegan butter; stir to combine. Add sliced onions and stir to coat. Cover and cook for 15 minutes, until soft and translucent, stirring and checking often to ensure they do not burn. Add 1/2 tsp (2 mL) sea salt and cook, uncovered, stirring often, for 10 minutes, until onions are very soft and brown in color.

5. Stir in flour; cook, whisking constantly, for 3 minutes, until a thick paste forms. You may need to add more vegan butter to moisten the flour. Stir in 1 cup (250 mL) broth; cook, whisking constantly, for about 3 minutes, until smooth. Add remaining broth, wine and sage, and bring to a boil over high heat. Immediately reduce heat to medium-low and simmer for 30 minutes. Stir occasionally.

6. Brush baguette slices with olive oil on both sides and place on prepared baking sheet. Toast in the preheated oven for 20 minutes, flipping halfway through, until golden brown. Set aside.

FINE-MESH SIEVE
BAKING SHEET LINED WITH
  PARCHMENT PAPER
4 OVENPROOF SOUP BOWLS
RIMMED BAKING SHEET

10 cups water 2.5 L
Sea salt
1 cup dried porcini mushrooms 250 mL
1 cup dried oyster mushrooms 250 mL
1 cup dried shiitake mushrooms 250 mL
2 carrots, coarsely chopped 2
2 celery stalks, coarsely chopped 2
2 tbsp soy sauce or tamari 30 mL
2 tbsp vegan Worcestershire 30 mL
1/4 cup nutritional yeast 60 mL
2 bay leaves 2
1 tbsp dried thyme 15 mL
2 tsp black peppercorns 10 mL
2 garlic cloves, crushed 2
1/3 cup olive oil, divided 75 mL
3 tbsp vegan butter (approx.) 45 mL
3 large onions, sliced into thin half-moons 3
3 tbsp unbleached all-purpose flour 45 mL
1 cup red wine 250 mL
1 tsp ground dried sage 5 mL
1/2 baguette, sliced 1/2
Olive oil for brushing
Freshly ground black pepper
2 to 3 tbsp cognac (optional) 30 to 45 mL
1/2 onion, grated 1/2
Fondue Cheese (page 178)

7. Season soup with sea salt and pepper to taste. Add cognac, if using, and grated onion; stir to combine. Set the oven to Broil and place four ovenproof soup bowls on a rimmed baking sheet.

8. Spread a generous amount of fondue cheese onto one side of each baguette slice and ladle soup into bowls. Top each bowl with 1 to 2 baguette slices, and place the baking sheet under preheated broiler for 2 to 3 minutes, until cheese becomes bubbly and crispy around the edges. Remove from oven and serve immediately, with extra toasted baguette on the side.

Not-Boring Salads

/nät ˈbôriNG ˈsaləd/   *noun*

1. the opposite of a dull, uninteresting or #basic dish consisting of raw greens and vegetables, a dressing and — optionally — some form of protein (usually raw tofu) • *Tim hates vegetables, so I've tricked him into eating more greens with these lit not-boring salads.*

LET'S GET ONE THING STRAIGHT: salads bore me. I'd rather eat my own arm than watch James's cringing face as he pathetically picks at a handful of greens. I've found that salads with lots of hearty good stuff loaded on top are the key to hiding something you *actually* want to eat underneath.

Cobb Your Enthusiasm Salad

SERVES 4

Do you ever find yourself looking down into a bowl of greens and thinking to yourself, "I'd rather be fat?" If so, this is the salad for you! Like the original, our cobb is full of robust flavors — seasoned hearts of palm, chunky bits of protein, creamy avocado and salty mushroom bacon, with a tangy mustard vinaigrette. It's the salad that eats like a meal!

1. **Tangy Mustard Dressing:** In a small bowl or mason jar, combine red wine vinegar, olive oil, mustard, garlic, lemon juice, maple syrup, sea salt and pepper; whisk or shake to combine. Taste and adjust sea salt and pepper as needed. Set aside.

2. **Salad:** In a medium bowl, toss hearts of palm and black salt.

3. In another medium bowl, whisk together nutritional yeast and 1/8 tsp (0.5 mL) turmeric. Add more turmeric (up to 1/8 tsp/0.5 mL) until the color resembles an egg yolk. Add half the hearts of palm; mash with a fork and toss until completely coated and a soft yellow color. Transfer back to the first bowl and toss gently to create what looks like a chopped hard-boiled egg. (If you toss it too much, the yellow will overpower the white areas). Set aside.

4. In a medium skillet, heat coconut oil over medium heat. Add chicken-substitute strips and cook for about 5 to 8 minutes, until heated through and slightly golden brown.

5. On a large platter or in a wide salad bowl, toss romaine and spinach to mix. Arrange bacon bits, hearts of palm, avocados, chicken strips and tomato on top of greens in neat rows or sections. Drizzle with desired amount of dressing and garnish with chives and dill.

~~ HACK IT! ~~

To make this recipe quick and easy, use store-bought vegan chicken substitute or leftover seitan you have in the fridge or freezer. If you're free as a bird for time, make our Become a Master of Seitan: Chicken (Breasts, page 39) from scratch and cut it into strips.

TANGY MUSTARD DRESSING
1/4 cup red wine vinegar 60 mL
1/2 cup extra virgin olive oil 125 mL
2 tbsp Dijon mustard 30 mL
1 garlic clove, minced 1
1 tbsp freshly squeezed lemon juice 15 mL
1-1/2 tbsp pure maple syrup 22 mL
1/2 tsp sea salt (approx.) 2 mL
1/2 tsp freshly ground black pepper (approx.) 2 mL

SALAD
2 cups drained and chopped hearts of palm 500 mL
1/2 tsp black salt or sea salt 2 mL
2 tbsp nutritional yeast 30 mL
1/8 to 1/4 tsp ground turmeric 0.5 to 1 mL
1 tbsp coconut oil 15 mL
2 cups chicken substitute of choice, cut into strips 500 mL
1 head romaine lettuce, shredded 1
2 cups chopped spinach 500 mL
1 cup chopped Mushroom Bacon (page 46) 250 mL
2 ripe avocados, diced 2
1 tomato, seeded and chopped 1
2 tbsp chopped fresh chives 30 mL
2 tbsp chopped fresh dill 30 mL

Deconstructed Pizza

SERVES 4

It's a pizza! It's a salad! It's a pizza salad! Not so long ago, in the lead up to our wedding both of us went on a diet. But 98 percent of the time we both want pizza, so this is a happy compromise. It has all the flavors you love in a pizza, but is served as a yummy, good-for-your-tummy *and* your taste buds salad. Wedding diet approved.

1. In a medium bowl, whisk together 2 minced garlic cloves, thyme, pepper, fennel seeds and 2 tbsp (30 mL) olive oil. Add tomatoes and gently toss to coat.

2. Arrange tomatoes in a single layer, cut side up, on baking sheet and sprinkle with any leftover olive oil from the bowl. Bake in preheated oven for 1-1/2 hours, until soft and slightly deflated. Remove from oven and set aside.

3. Raise the oven temperature to 400°F (200°C).

4. In a large bowl, whisk together 3 tbsp (45 mL) olive oil and 1/4 tsp (1 mL) sea salt. Add bread and toss to coat. Spread bread on a baking sheet in a single layer and bake for about 15 minutes, until slightly golden brown.

5. In a blender, combine 1 cup (250 mL) basil, 1 garlic clove, 1/4 cup (60 mL) olive oil, lemon juice and 1/2 tsp (2 mL) sea salt; blend on High until smooth. Taste and adjust sea salt and pepper as needed. Set aside.

6. In a large salad bowl, combine romaine lettuce and the remaining 1/2 cup (125 mL) basil; add dressing and toss to coat. Add roasted tomatoes, bread cubes, banana peppers and nutritional yeast; toss to combine.

HACK IT!

I **sometimes add chunks** of vegan Parmesan or any other vegan cheese I have lying around. For obvious reasons, it really makes that pizza flavor pop!

PREHEAT OVEN TO 300°F (150°C)
2 BAKING SHEETS LINED WITH PARCHMENT PAPER
BLENDER

3 garlic cloves, minced and divided

1/2 tsp dried thyme 2 mL

1/2 tsp freshly ground black pepper 2 mL

1/2 tsp fennel seeds, crushed 2 mL

1/2 cup + 2 tsp extra virgin olive oil, divided 135 mL

1 lb cherry tomatoes, halved 500 g

Sea salt

1-1/2 cups fresh basil, chopped and divided 375 mL

1 tbsp freshly squeezed lemon juice 15 mL

Freshly ground black pepper

1 head romaine lettuce, cut into bite-size pieces 1

1/4 baguette, cubed 1/4

1/4 cup drained pickled banana peppers 60 mL

2 tbsp nutritional yeast 30 mL

Naked Burrito

SERVES 4

Yes, Chipotle, I am fully aware that the guac costs extra. **This is a magical homemade burrito bowl without arbitrary guac limitations, and it makes for delicious meal prep. Make a big batch on Sunday, and you've got yummy lunches for days.**

1. **Rice:** Rinse rice in a fine-mesh sieve. In a medium saucepan, bring water to a boil. Stir in rice, oil and sea salt; immediately reduce heat to low. Cover with a tight-fitting lid and simmer for 30 minutes, until all the water has been absorbed. The rice should be tender. If it's a bit uncooked and crunchy, add a little more water and continue cooking for up to 10 minutes, until rice is done. Remove from heat, cover and set aside.

2. **Beans:** In a small saucepan, heat coconut oil over medium heat. Stir in garlic, chili powder, oregano, cumin and onion powder; cook, stirring, for about 1 minute, until fragrant. Add beans (do not drain) and cook, stirring often, for 20 minutes, until heated through and thickened.

3. **Chili Lime Corn Salsa:** In a medium bowl, combine corn, onion, chili powder, cilantro and lime juice. Season with sea salt and pepper. Add more chili powder if you love the heat! Set aside.

4. **Fajita Peppers:** In a medium skillet, heat coconut oil over medium heat. Add garlic and onion; sauté for 3 minutes, until translucent. Add cumin and chili powder; sauté for 1 minute or until fragrant. Add red pepper, green pepper, sea salt, pepper and water; cover and cook for 5 minutes, until peppers soften. Remove cover and cook, stirring occasionally, for an additional 5 minutes, or until onion begins to brown. Set aside.

5. **Chicken:** In another medium skillet, heat coconut oil over medium heat. Add paprika, cumin and oregano; cook, stirring constantly for 1 minute, until fragrant. Add chicken substitute and cook, stirring, for about 5 minutes, until heated through.

6. **To build:** Fluff rice with a spoon or a fork, then divide between four bowls. Top each with a handful of romaine lettuce, black beans, fajita peppers, chicken, salsa, sour cream and mashed avocado. Sprinkle some green onion and cilantro on top. Serve with tortilla chips on the side.

FINE-MESH SIEVE

RICE
1 cup brown rice 250 mL
2-1/2 cups water 625 mL
1 tsp olive oil 5 mL
1/2 tsp sea salt 2 mL

BEANS
1 tbsp coconut oil 15 mL
1 garlic clove, minced 1
1/2 tsp chili powder 2 mL
1/2 tsp dried oregano 2 mL
1/2 tsp ground cumin 2 mL
1 tsp onion powder 5 mL
1 can (14 oz/398 mL) black beans, with liquid 1

CHILI LIME CORN SALSA
(page 103)

FAJITA PEPPERS
1 tbsp coconut oil 15 mL
1 garlic clove, minced 1
1/2 small red onion, cut into half-moons 1/2
1 tsp ground cumin 5 mL
1/4 tsp chili powder 1 mL
1 red bell pepper, sliced 1
1 green bell pepper, sliced 1
1/2 tsp sea salt 2 mL
1/4 tsp freshly ground black pepper 1 mL
2 tbsp water 30 mL

CHICKEN
1 tbsp coconut oil 15 mL
1/2 tsp paprika 2 mL
1/2 tsp ground cumin 2 mL
1/2 tsp dried oregano 2 mL
2 cups chicken substitute of choice, cut into strips 500 mL

ACCOUTREMENTS
1/4 head romaine lettuce, shredded 1/4
1 cup Burrito-Worthy Sour Cream (page 51) 250 mL
1 avocado, mashed 1
1 green onion, sliced 1
Tortilla chips

CHILI LIME CORN SALSA
1 can (14 oz/398 mL) sweet corn, drained and rinsed 1
1/2 small red onion, diced 1/2
1/8 tsp chili powder (approx.) 0.5 mL
1/4 cup fresh cilantro, finely chopped 60 mL
Juice of 1/2 lime
Sea salt and freshly ground black pepper

The Buffalo Caesar

SERVES 4

What's so great about Caesar, huh? Buffalo is just as good as Caesar. Buffalo is just as loved as Caesar. People totally like buffalo just as much as they like Caesar. When did it become okay for one sauce to be the boss of everybody? That's not what salad is about! We should totally just add buffalo to Caesar!

1. **Caesar Dressing:** In a blender, combine cashews and water; blend on High until creamy. Add olive oil, 1 tbsp (15 mL) nutritional yeast, lemon juice, mustard, capers, garlic, soy sauce and kelp, if using. Blend until smooth. (If dressing is too thick, add more water, a little bit at a time. If it's too thin, you can add more cashews or 1/2 tsp/2 mL chia seeds to help thicken it.) It should resemble traditional Caesar salad dressing. Season to taste with sea salt and pepper and set aside.

2. **Buffalo Salad:** In a large bowl, toss cauliflower in buffalo sauce. Set aside.

3. In another large bowl, combine romaine lettuce, bacon, if using, and the remaining 2 tbsp (30 mL) nutritional yeast; add dressing and toss to coat. The amount of dressing you use is up to you: some love their salad lightly dressed, and others like it sauce-heavy.

4. Divide between four salad plates and top with equal amounts of cauliflower or chicken substitute. Serve with a lemon wedge.

∼ HACK IT! ∼

To make this recipe in a hurry, use store-bought vegan chicken substitute or leftover seitan you have in the fridge or freezer. If you're free as a bird for time, make our Become a Master of Seitan: Chicken (Breasts, page 39) from scratch and cut it into strips.

Wrap each serving in a tortilla and enjoy as a wrap. It's a no-mess way to eat salad with your hands!

Store leftover dressing in a container in the fridge for up to 5 days.

BLENDER

CAESAR DRESSING

1/2 cup raw cashews, soaked overnight and rinsed (see page 26) 125 mL

1/3 cup water 75 mL

1 tbsp olive oil 15 mL

3 tbsp nutritional yeast, divided 45 mL

Juice of 1/2 lemon

1 tsp Dijon mustard 5 mL

1-1/2 tbsp minced drained capers 22 mL

1 garlic clove, crushed 1

1 tbsp soy sauce or tamari 15 mL

1 tsp kelp granules (optional) 5 mL

Sea salt and freshly ground black pepper

BUFFALO SALAD

4 cups Buffalo Cauliflower Wings (page 138) or chicken substitute of choice, cut into strips 1 L

1/3 cup Buffalo Sauce (page 140) 75 mL

2 heads romaine lettuce, ripped into bite-size pieces 2

1/2 cup chopped Eggplant Bacon (page 48; optional) 125 mL

1 lemon, cut into wedges 1

It Takes Two to Mango

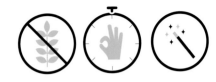

SERVES 4 AS A SIDE OR 2 AS A MAIN

Did you know that in Thailand it is illegal to leave your house without underwear on? Luckily, this takeout favourite is easily made in the comfort of your own home. It's the perfect combination of all five Thai flavors: sweet, sour, spicy, salty and bitter. I recommend enjoying it while working from home without pants on.

1. In a small skillet, toast peanuts over medium-high heat for about 6 to 8 minutes, until fragrant and golden. Set aside.

2. In a large, shallow bowl, toss mangos, red pepper, bean sprouts, red chile, green onions, shallot, cilantro and basil.

3. In a small bowl, whisk together garlic, sesame oil, soy sauce, maple syrup, chili sauce and lime juice. Pour over salad and toss to coat. Add toasted peanuts and additional basil and cilantro to garnish. Serve as a starter for Street Food–Style Thai Basil Beef (page 191)

HACK IT!

Use tamari to make this dish gluten-free!

Add protein to this salad by topping it with seitan slices or your favorite chicken substitute.

1/2 cup crushed peanuts 125 mL
2 mangos, sliced lengthwise 2
1 red bell pepper, sliced lengthwise 1
1/2 cup bean sprouts 125 mL
1 red Thai chile, sliced 1
2 green onions, chopped 2
1 shallot, thinly sliced 1
1/2 cup fresh cilantro, finely chopped 125 mL
1/2 cup fresh Thai basil, finely chopped 125 mL
1 garlic clove, minced 1
2 tbsp sesame oil 30 mL
2 tbsp soy sauce or tamari 30 mL
2 tbsp pure maple syrup 30 mL
1/4 tsp Asian chili sauce 1 mL
1 tbsp freshly squeezed lime juice 15 mL
Fresh finely chopped basil
Fresh finely chopped cilantro

French Bistro Salad

SERVES 4

This salad is my veganized version of a *frisée aux lardons*. It's hollandaise and bacon on top of salad. Need I say more?

1. In a small bowl, whisk together lemon juice, mustard, shallot, 1/4 tsp (1 mL) sea salt, pepper and 1/4 cup (60 mL) olive oil. Set aside.

2. Pour the remaining 1/4 cup (60 mL) olive oil into a small bowl. Using a pastry brush, brush a small amount of oil on each side of bread slices and place on a prepared baking sheet. Toast slices in the preheated oven for 7 to 12 minutes, flipping halfway, until crispy and golden brown.

3. Remove from oven and rub garlic cloves over each crostini. Set aside.

4. Place frisée in a large bowl; lightly salt and toss with vinaigrette to coat. Divide greens between four plates and top with bacon bits.

5. Spread a thick layer of hollandaise on each piece of toasted baguette and place two in the center of each plate of greens. Shower with freshly ground black pepper and serve.

HACK IT!

I love to eat this salad like an open-face sandwich, spooning the greens over the baguette slices and using the extra to sop up the remaining dressing.

Try this salad topped with some fried tofu.

PREHEAT OVEN TO 400°F (200°C)
BAKING SHEET LINED WITH PARCHMENT PAPER
BLENDER

2 tbsp freshly squeezed lemon juice 30 mL

1 tbsp Dijon mustard 15 mL

1 shallot, minced 1

Sea salt

1/4 tsp freshly ground pepper 1 mL

1/2 cup extra virgin olive oil, divided 125 mL

1/4 baguette, sliced diagonally 1/4

2 garlic cloves, halved, with skin 2

7 cups frisée (French curly endive) 1.75 L

8 slices Eggplant Bacon (page 48), cut into chunks 8

1/2 cup Ritzy Hollandaise (page 53), at room temperature 125 mL

Freshly ground black pepper

The Token Kale Salad

SERVES 4 AS A SIDE OR 2 AS A MAIN

As the saying goes, "You don't make friends with salad" — until you do. This kale and pesto salad is so beyond run-of-the-mill. Pasta sauce on salad? Why didn't anyone think of this earlier? It's a match made in BFF heaven. It's delicious on its own, but let's face it: salad is a sad meal, so pair it with a burger (pages 209 to 213) or a hearty bowl of Half-Baked Mac and Cheese (page 170). Now, that's what I call balance.

1. In a large bowl, drizzle kale with olive oil and massage leaves with your hands. Add pesto and continue to massage, until kale is completely coated. Add tomatoes, red pepper and red onion to salad. Sprinkle with nutritional yeast, hemp seeds and sea salt and pepper to taste. Toss well to combine and top with cashews to serve.

HACK IT!

It might seem a bit strange to massage your food, but you'll be amazed at what a quick five-minute rubdown can do. Take handfuls of kale and rub them together. Play some spa music, for the full effect. As you massage, you will start to notice the leaves getting darker in color and becoming silky in texture. The longer you massage your kale, the more it will break down and become less bitter. Massage kale with pesto or dressing of choice and refrigerate up to 48 hours in advance.

4 cups shredded dinosaur kale 1 L
2 tbsp extra virgin olive oil 30 mL
1-1/2 cups Presto, Pesto (page 54) 375 mL
1/2 cup grape tomatoes, halved 125 mL
1/2 cup diced red bell pepper 125 mL
1/4 cup finely diced red onion 60 mL
2 tbsp nutritional yeast 30 mL
1 tbsp hemp seeds 15 mL
Sea salt and freshly ground black pepper
1/4 cup chopped cashews 60 mL

Eat the Rainbow . . . Slaw

MAKES 4 TO 6 SIDE SERVINGS

I've never met a slaw I wanted to eat. A good slaw is like a unicorn — it's almost impossible to find. *Yes, almost, because unicorns are real; you just haven't seen one.* This colorful, light slaw has the just right amount of zing. It's hearty enough to serve on its own, and it adds a fresh sparkle to Baja Fish Tacos (page 177) and Shredded Hogtown Jackfruit (page 199).

1. In a small bowl, whisk together apple cider vinegar, mayo, maple syrup, celery seeds, mustard powder, dill, cayenne and 1/4 tsp (1 mL) each sea salt and pepper.

2. In a large bowl, toss together purple cabbage, green cabbage, carrots, green onions and red onion. Toss with dressing until evenly coated. Season to taste with sea salt and pepper. Transfer to the fridge for a minimum of 30 minutes and up to 2 hours, to allow the flavors to meld before serving.

∼ HACK IT! ∼

I use my food processor to shred everything, so the cabbage is ready in a flash. I refuse to shred or grate by hand — ain't nobody got time for that!

2 tbsp apple cider vinegar 30 mL
3/4 cup Hell No! Egg-Free Mayo (page 50) 175 mL
1-1/2 tsp pure maple syrup 7 mL
1 tsp celery seeds 5 mL
1 tsp dry mustard powder 5 mL
1 tbsp finely chopped fresh dill 15 mL
1/8 tsp cayenne pepper 0.5 mL
Sea salt and freshly ground black pepper
1 small purple cabbage, shredded 1
1 small green cabbage, shredded 1
2 large carrots, grated 2
3 green onions, sliced on the bias 3
1/2 small red onion, finely chopped 1/2

Grandma Leyla's Fattoush

SERVES 4 AS A SIDE

According to James, no one makes food as well as his Syrian grandmother. *Obviously he is mistaken, and he has forgotten that his grandmother and wife are tied for that position.* I've got to hand it to her — this vibrant salad, rich in fresh Mediterranean veggies, a large sprinkling of parsley and the fun crunch of fried pita, gives me a feeling of both indulgence and health that I just can't find anywhere else. Grandma Leyla is really on to something.

1. In a colander, sprinkle eggplant with 1/2 tsp (2 mL) sea salt; toss to coat. Let stand for 25 minutes, then blot excess moisture with paper towel.

2. In a large, deep, heavy-bottomed saucepan, heat 2 to 3 inches (5 to 7.5 cm) vegetable oil over medium-high heat until temperate registers 325°F (160°C) on a deep-fry thermometer.

3. In batches, fry pita cubes in hot oil for about 1 minute, until golden brown. Using a slotted spoon, remove pita chips, shake off excess oil and blot dry with paper towel.

4. Place eggplant cubes in a large bowl and drizzle evenly with 2 tbsp (30 mL) olive oil. Add cumin and toss to coat. Sprinkle with a pinch of sea salt and 1/4 tsp (1 mL) pepper. Place eggplant on a prepared baking sheet in a single layer. Bake in the preheated oven for 10 minutes, flip and continue to roast for 20 minutes, until tender and caramelized.

5. In a small bowl, whisk together 1/4 cup (60 mL) olive oil, garlic, 1/4 tsp (1 mL) sea salt, lemon juice and 1/4 tsp (1 mL) pepper. Set aside.

6. In a large bowl, combine onion, parsley, tomatoes, cucumber and romaine lettuce; toss with dressing. Add pita chips; toss gently to combine. Adjust sea salt and pepper to taste. This salad pairs really well with Why So Syrian Chicken and Rice (page 158) and a vat of hummus!

PREHEAT OVEN TO 425°F (220°C)
LARGE, DEEP, HEAVY-BOTTOMED SAUCEPAN
DEEP-FRY THERMOMETER
BAKING SHEET LINED WITH PARCHMENT PAPER

---

1 large eggplant, cut into cubes 1
Sea salt
Vegetable oil for frying
2 pieces Lebanese-style pita, cubed 2
6 tbsp olive oil, divided 90 mL
1 tsp ground cumin 5 mL
Freshly ground black pepper
2 garlic cloves, minced 2
1 tbsp freshly squeezed lemon juice 15 mL
1 small red onion, finely chopped 1
1 cup curly parsley, finely chopped 250 mL
2 plum (Roma) tomatoes, diced and seeds removed 2
1/2 cucumber, diced 1/2
1/4 head romaine lettuce, shredded 1/4

Munchies

/ˈmən(t)SHē/   *noun*   *informal*   **munchie**

1. a small item of food suitable for snacking.

plural noun: **the munchies**
1. a sudden intense desire for snack food.
2. the consumption of extensive amounts of carbohydrates and polyunsaturated fats following inhaling the byproducts of combusting the hemp plant. • *"I got some badass munchies. Better break out the Oreos."*

THE BEAUTY OF MUNCHIES IS THAT THEY ARE GOOD AT ANY TIME. Seriously, when isn't a good time for a samosa? Under what circumstance is it NOT okay to scarf down some chile lime cashews? These are perfect for literally any situation, whether you're hosting a Superbowl party or a girls' night to watch reruns of *Sex and the City* (I'm totally a Carrie, btw) or need to satisfy that 2 a.m. craving. (And the 4:19 p.m. craving, too!)

Doses of Samosas

MAKES 12 SAMOSAS

Ordering Indian is a weekly ritual for us on evenings when all we can manage is watching reruns of *Law & Order: SVU*. Our favorite spot is a vegan-friendly roti place with out-of-this-world samosas. It took me months to crack their secret recipe, but I finally managed to nail down these perfectly fried folded triangles of herb-essenced, potato goodness.

1. In a large bowl, whisk together flour, onion seeds, black salt, if using, and 1/2 tsp (2 mL) sea salt. Make a well in the center of the bowl and add olive oil. Using your fingers, massage oil into the flour, until mixture resembles dusty crumbles.

2. Add water, 1 tbsp (15 mL) at a time, and knead to make a soft and firm but pliable dough (you may not need all the water or you may need to add more flour or water). Knead for 5 minutes, cover with plastic wrap and set aside for 1 hour or up to 8 hours.

3. Meanwhile, place potatoes in a medium saucepan and fill with water. Bring to a boil, then immediately reduce to medium heat and boil gently for 15 minutes, or until potatoes are easily pierced with a fork. Drain and set aside.

4. In a large skillet, heat coriander seeds and cumin seeds over medium-high heat. Dry-roast, stirring constantly, for about 3 to 5 minutes, until fragrant. Remove from heat and transfer to a mortar; grind with a pestle until smooth. Set aside.

5. Using the same pan, heat peanut oil over medium-high heat. Add chili powder, ground coriander, turmeric and garam masala; toast, stirring constantly, for 1 minute, until fragrant. Add ginger, onion and chiles; sauté for about 3 to 5 minutes, until onion is translucent. Add potatoes and cook for about 5 minutes, until they begin to brown slightly. Mash slightly with a fork. Mix in peas, spices from the mortar and 1 tsp (5 mL) sea salt; cook, stirring, for 3 to 5 minutes, until heated through. Remove from heat. Season with sea salt to taste and lemon juice. Stir in cilantro and set aside to cool.

6. In a deep fryer or heavy-bottomed saucepan, heat vegetable oil to 375°F (190°C). If you are frying on the stove, you'll need roughly 2 to 3 inches (5 to 7.5 cm) of oil.

MORTAR AND PESTLE
DEEP FRYER OR
 HEAVY-BOTTOMED SAUCE-
PAN FITTED WITH A DEEP-
FRY THERMOMETER
ROLLING PIN
ICE CREAM SCOOP
 (OPTIONAL)

2 cups unbleached all-purpose flour (approx.) 500 mL

1 tsp onion seeds 5 mL

1/4 tsp black salt (optional) 1 mL

Sea salt

1/4 cup olive oil 60 mL

1/2 cup lukewarm water (approx.) 125 mL

4 yellow-flesh potatoes, peeled and halved 4

1 tbsp coriander seeds 15 mL

1 tsp cumin seeds 5 mL

2 tbsp peanut oil 30 mL

1 tbsp chili powder 15 mL

1 tsp ground coriander 5 mL

1/4 tsp ground turmeric 1 mL

1/2 tsp garam masala 2 mL

1 tbsp minced fresh ginger 15 mL

1 small onion, diced 1

1 green Thai chile, finely chopped 1

1/4 cup fresh or frozen sweet green peas 60 mL

1 tsp freshly squeezed lemon juice 5 mL

1/4 cup fresh cilantro, finely chopped 60 mL

Unbleached all-purpose flour for dusting

Vegetable oil for frying

Mango or tamarind chutney

7. On a lightly floured surface, using a sharp knife, cut dough into six equal pieces.

8. Gently shape dough pieces into balls and place all but one in a large bowl; cover with plastic wrap.

9. Using a rolling pin, roll out one piece of dough into a very thin oval shape. Cut oval in half and make a cone shape by folding the cut edge in half and pinching the edges together. Use a small amount of water to help make the seal. Using a large ice cream scoop or spoon, place about one-twelfth of the potato filling in cone, and gently pinch dough closed with wet fingertips. It should form a triangle. Ensure that all the sides are sealed, and press the tines of a fork along the edges of the triangle to form a decorative pattern. Repeat until you run out of dough.

10. Deep-fry 2 or 3 samosas at time for 4 to 5 minutes, until golden brown. Using a slotted spoon, remove from oil and place on a plate lined with paper towel. Let cool for 5 minutes. Serve warm, with mango or tamarind chutney for dipping.

HACK IT!

Adjust the heat by adding more or less green chiles.

Worried about bathing suit season? Simply cook the samosas on a baking sheet lined with parchment paper in a 350°F (180°C) oven for 30 to 35 minutes instead of deep-frying, and you have a low-fat snack! #MadeIt

Store wrapped leftovers in the fridge for 5 to 7 days or in the freezer for up to 1 month.

Szechuan-Style Pan-Fried Dumplings

MAKES ROUGHLY 32 DUMPLINGS

There are plenty of magical hangover cures posted all over the Internet, but nothing is as effective as all-you-can-eat dumplings. Every New Year's Day, we head to our favorite spot in Chinatown to lick our wounds and the plates. This mouthwatering veggie take on a traditional Chinese dumpling is filled with a meaty bok choy that is super juicy and delicious.

1. **Hunan Sauce:** In a small bowl, whisk together peanut butter, soy sauce, sesame oil, rice vinegar, garlic and chili paste. Add hot water 2 tbsp (30 mL) at a time, whisking constantly, until thin but not runny. Add additional soy sauce and sesame oil to taste. Set aside.

2. **Spicy Sesame Sauce:** In a small bowl, whisk together soy sauce, chili paste, rice vinegar and sesame oil. Adjust soy sauce and chili paste to taste. Set aside.

3. **Dumpling Dough:** In a large bowl, whisk together flour and sea salt. Add 1 cup (250 mL) hot water and mix with a wooden spoon to form a dough. On a lightly floured surface, knead dough for 5 minutes, until smooth. The dough should be soft and spring back when touched. Place dough in a large bowl and cover with a damp cloth. Let stand for about 1 hour.

4. **Filling:** In a large wok or skillet, heat sesame oil over medium-high heat. Sauté garlic and ginger for about 2 minutes, until fragrant. Add bok choy and soy sauce; sauté for about 5 to 8 minutes, until greens are wilted, stalks are tender but crisp and most of the liquid in the skillet has evaporated. Remove from heat; mix in seitan and chives. Season to taste with sea salt and set aside.

5. Cut dough into four equal pieces. On a lightly floured surface, roll each piece of dough into a snake, about 10 to 15 inches (25 to 37.5 cm) long. Dust snakes with flour if dough is sticking. Cut each snake into eight equal pieces and return to bowl. Repeat with remaining snakes and cover with the damp cloth.

6. Take out one dough piece at a time and roll it into a circle roughly 3 to 4 inches (7.5 to 10 cm) in diameter. You want the outside perimeter to be thinner than the center, but

---

PASTRY BLENDER
(OPTIONAL)
PASTRY CLOTH (OPTIONAL)
BAKING SHEET LINED WITH
PARCHMENT PAPER

HUNAN SAUCE

1/3 cup creamy natural peanut butter 75 mL

2 tbsp soy sauce or tamari (approx.) 30 mL

2 tbsp toasted sesame oil (approx.) 30 mL

1 tbsp seasoned rice vinegar 15 mL

1 garlic clove, minced 1

1 tsp Asian chili paste (like gochujang) or Sriracha sauce 5 mL

1/4 cup hot water (approx.) 60 mL

SPICY SESAME SAUCE

1/4 cup soy sauce or tamari 60 mL

1-1/2 tbsp Asian chili paste (like gochujang) or Sriracha sauce 22 mL

1 tbsp seasoned rice vinegar 15 mL

1 tbsp toasted sesame oil 15 mL

DUMPLING DOUGH

2 cups unbleached all-purpose flour 500 mL

1 tsp sea salt 5 mL

1 cup hot water 250 mL

Unbleached all-purpose flour for dusting

(Ingredients continue on page 123)

not by much. Spoon 1 tbsp (15 mL) filling into the middle and wet the edge with a little water. Fold up two sides of the dough so that it looks like a taco and, starting at one end, pinch to seal, working your way along the edge to the middle. Pull the opposite end of the taco toward the middle to meet the pinched section and form a flat-bottomed triangle (aka a pyramid); pinch the remaining two sides to seal, squeezing out air as you enclose the filling. Place on a baking sheet. Repeat with each dumpling piece and filling.

7. In a large skillet, heat 3 tbsp (45 mL) peanut oil over medium-high heat. Once oil begins to shimmer, place half the dumplings in the pan, flat side down, and cook for 3 minutes, until just beginning to brown slightly. Pour 1/2 cup (125 mL) water into the skillet, cover and steam for 7 to 10 minutes, until the water evaporates. Remove cover, reduce heat to low and cook, moving the pan constantly to prevent sticking, for about 2 minutes, until bottoms are golden, tops are translucent and filling is heated through. Transfer to a warmed serving dish or platter. Repeat with the remaining dumplings, reheating the pan over medium-high heat before adding the remaining peanut oil. Serve with Hunan and spicy sesame sauces on the side for dipping.

~~ HACK IT! ~~

Homemade dumpling dough is great, but sometimes a girl gets lazy — that's what premade wonton wrappers are for! You can find them at Asian supermarkets or in the international section of the grocery store.

Here's an idea! Double the recipe and freeze for a quick dinner on lazy days. Dust each dumpling with flour to prevent sticking and stack, separating the layers with parchment. Wrap them in a few layers of plastic wrap and slide stacks into heavy-duty freezer bags. Freeze for up to 3 months. To cook, allow wrapped dumplings to come to room temperature, then proceed with Step 7.

FILLING

2 tbsp toasted sesame oil 30 mL
3 garlic cloves, minced 3
1 1-inch (2.5 cm) piece fresh ginger, grated 1
5 large bok choy heads, chopped 5
2 tbsp soy sauce or tamari 30 mL
2 cups minced Seitan Mastery: Beef 2.0 (Hack It! page 40) 500 mL
1/4 cup finely chopped fresh chives 60 mL
Sea salt

6 tbsp peanut or vegetable oil, divided 90 mL
1 cup water, divided 250 mL

Jalapeño Poppin'

MAKES 15 POPPERS

There are no words to describe our love for hot peppers, and there is no better way to rationalize eating five jalapeños in one sitting than by serving poppers. These spicy but creamy and cheesy peppers wrapped in crispy breading are so addictive they really should come with a warning. Serve with a side of Austin-Tacious Roasted Salsa (page 150), aioli (page 59) or Burrito-Worthy Sour Cream (page 57) for the perfect appetizer.

1. In a medium bowl, whisk together eggless dip and egg replacer until smooth. Set aside.

2. In a deep fryer or heavy-bottomed saucepan, heat vegetable oil to 375°F (190°C). If you are frying on the stove, you'll need at least 3 inches (7.5 cm) of oil.

3. In another medium bowl, combine vegan cream cheese, vegan Cheddar cheese, hot sauce and garlic powder. Set aside.

4. In a third medium bowl, whisk together bread crumbs, flour, oregano, paprika, sea salt and pepper. Set aside.

5. Cut a slit lengthwise from the stem to the bottom on one side of each pepper. With a small knife, remove seeds and veins. Using a small spoon, fill peppers with cheese mixture and press seams closed.

6. Dip jalapeños in eggless dip, then coat with breadcrumb mixture. Fry, in batches, for about 6 to 7 minutes, until golden brown. Remove from fryer and transfer to a plate lined with paper towel. Let cool for 5 minutes and serve.

DEEP FRYER OR HEAVY-BOTTOMED SAUCEPAN FITTED WITH A DEEP-FRY THERMOMETER

1 recipe Eggcellent Eggless Dip (page 35) 1

1-1/2 tbsp powdered egg replacer (I like Ener-G) 22 mL

Vegetable oil for frying

1 cup vegan cream cheese or It's a Bella Mozzarella (page 37) 250 mL

1/2 cup vegan Cheddar cheese shreds 125 mL

1 tsp hot sauce 5 mL

1/2 tsp garlic powder 2 mL

1/2 cup panko bread crumbs 125 mL

1/2 cup unbleached all-purpose flour 125 mL

1 tbsp dried oregano 15 mL

1 tsp paprika 5 mL

1/4 tsp sea salt 1 mL

1/4 tsp freshly ground black pepper 1 mL

12 jalapeño peppers 12

Chile Lime Cashews

MAKES 2 CUPS (500 ML)

What sound does a nut makes when it sneezes? *Ca-SHEW!* The most hilarious kitchen nightmare to date has been trying to recreate Trader Joe's famous chile lime cashews. After converting hundreds of dollars worth of cashews into coal, few snacks are more satisfying than these fragrant, spiced nuts.

1. In a coffee/spice grinder, pulse lemongrass, paprika, garlic powder, dried chiles and cayenne until a fine powder forms.

2. In a large bowl, whisk together lime zest, olive oil, lime juice and maple syrup. Add spice powder mixture and whisk until incorporated. Let stand for at least 2 minutes or up to 10 minutes. Add cashews and toss to coat. Add sea salt and toss again.

3. Spread cashews on a prepared baking sheet. Bake in the preheated oven, stirring every 5 minutes, for 20 to 25 minutes or until lightly golden. Be careful not to burn the nuts!

4. Lift parchment paper and transfer nuts to the counter for about 1 hour, until cooled completely. They should be fully dried, cool and a bit tacky to the touch. Serve to friends or down the whole recipe's worth on your own, like James does.

 *HACK IT!*

Only have raw cashews at home? (Or did you buy raw cashews by accident, like I did?) Stick them in the oven at 350°F (180°C) for 10 minutes or until golden, and presto — roasted cashews!

You can buy dried lemongrass at your local health food store or Asian grocery store. If you have a hard time finding dried leaves, lemongrass powder can be used in its place.

Store in a container at room temperature for up to 7 days.

PREHEAT OVEN TO 350°F (180°C)
COFFEE/SPICE GRINDER OR BLENDER
BAKING SHEET LINED WITH PARCHMENT PAPER

1 tsp dried lemongrass, finely chopped 5 mL

1 tsp paprika 5 mL

1 tsp garlic powder 5 mL

1 tbsp chopped dried red chiles or red pepper flakes 15 mL

1/8 tsp cayenne pepper 0.5 mL

1 tbsp grated lime zest (approx.) 15 mL

2 tbsp olive oil 30 mL

2-1/2 tbsp freshly squeezed lime juice 37 mL

2 tbsp + 2 tsp pure maple syrup 40 mL

2 cups roasted, unsalted cashews 500 mL

1-1/2 tsp coarse sea salt 7 mL

Theater Popcorn and Flavor Shakers

SERVES 4

I can easily stay up until 2 a.m. editing our next video or scrolling through Instagram, but put me in a movie theater and I'm asleep within 30 minutes. Maybe it's the dark setting, maybe it's good ol'-fashioned sleep deprivation. Either way, now we watch movies at home, where we can pause and whip up another batch of dill pickle popcorn.

1. In a stock pot, melt coconut oil over high heat. Immediately add popcorn kernels and shake the pot to coat completely. Let stand for about 15 seconds, then shake the pot constantly to avoid burning.

2. When you hear the first kernel pop, immediately put the lid on the pot. Leave a little opening for steam to escape. Continue to shake the pot constantly to prevent burning.

3. When the popping begins to slow, remove from heat and let stand for about 2 minutes, until the popping has stopped.

4. Slowly add vegan butter while tossing to coat completely. Season with salt or flavor shakers (pages 130 to 131) to taste.

1/4 cup coconut oil 60 mL
1 cup popcorn kernels 250 mL
1/2 cup vegan butter, melted 125 mL
Superfine salt

～～ HACK IT! ～～～～～～～～～～

Make superfine salt by running your normal sea salt through a blender, spice grinder or food processor until you end up with a fine powder.

DILL PICKLE

2 tbsp dried dill 30 mL
2 tbsp ground coriander 30 mL
1 tsp dry mustard powder 5 mL
1 tsp onion powder 5 mL
1 tsp garlic powder 5 mL
1 tsp celery seeds 5 mL
1 tbsp sea salt 15 mL
1 tsp citric acid powder (optional) 5 mL

Flavor Shakers

MAKES ABOUT 1/3 CUP (75 ML)

1.

In a coffee/spice grinder or blender, combine ingredients and pulse until you have fine powder. Sprinkle over popcorn while tossing, or leave out for guests to shake over their own portions.

~ HACK IT! ~

You can find citric acid powder at any health food store or in the supplement section of a drugstore or supermarket. It is a naturally occurring acid that exists in many fruits and vegetables, especially in citrus. It is often used as a flavoring and preserving agent in many foods. It also makes dill pickle seasoning the BOMB.

Store in small spice jars with shaker lids at room temperature for up to 3 months.

NACHO CHEESE

1/4 cup nutritional yeast 60 mL
1 tsp garlic powder 5 mL
1 tsp onion powder 5 mL
1 tbsp paprika 15 mL
1 tsp sea salt 5 mL
1/4 tsp ground turmeric 1 mL

CHILI CHEESE

1/4 cup nutritional yeast 60 mL
1 tbsp chili powder 15 mL
1/4 tsp garlic powder 1 mL
1/4 tsp onion powder 1 mL
1/2 tsp paprika 2 mL
1 tsp ground cumin 5 mL
1 tsp sea salt 5 mL
1/8 tsp cayenne pepper (optional) 0.5 mL

COOL RANCH

2 tbsp nutritional yeast 30 mL
1 tbsp dried parsley 15 mL
1 tbsp dried basil 15 mL
1 tsp dried dill 5 mL
1 tsp garlic powder 5 mL
1 tbsp onion powder 15 mL
1/4 tsp freshly ground black pepper 1 mL
1/2 tsp sea salt 2 mL

SALTED CHOCOLATE

1-1/2 tbsp packed brown
sugar or coconut sugar
22 mL
1 tbsp unsweetened cocoa
powder 15 mL
1/4 tsp ground cinnamon 1 mL
1/4 tsp sea salt 1 mL

Montreal Famous Poutine

SERVES 4 TO 6

Poutine is Canada's national culinary treasure, and I guarantee it's on every tourist's top 10 to-do list. I grew up in a small town where we bought it from a truck at the side of the road in paper takeout containers, with cheese and gravy dripping out the sides. Poutine was one of the first recipes I made vegan, and it always reminds this now city girl of her humble, small town upbringing.

1. Divide fries between four to six shallow bowls or plates. Spoon gravy over fries and drizzle with cheese sauce. Garnish with parsley, if using.

HACK IT!

Vegan cheese often needs some help to melt completely. If you're using store-bought vegan cheese, preheat the oven to Broil. Dish up the poutine in broiler-proof bowls, then place prepared poutine (without parsley) in the oven for 1 to 2 minutes to melt cheese. Garnish and serve.

When selecting store-bought vegan cheese, the brick version is more authentic than shreds. You can crumble one-quarter of a brick of cheese over the fries, and it will look and taste like melted cheese curds.

Kick your poutine up a notch by adding pulled jackfruit (page 199) and/or pickled jalapeños.

1 **recipe** Potatoes Served in the French Manner (page 224) 1

1 **recipe** Liquid Gold Gravy (page 56), warmed 1

1 **recipe** The Art of Cheese Sauce (page 52), warmed, or 1 cup (250 mL) crumbled vegan cheese 1

1/4 **cup** fresh parsley, chopped (optional) 60 mL

Kimchi Fries

SERVES 4

Two of our friends own a restaurant that's known for its pad thai fries, and I am completely obsessed with them. *Damn you, Kyla and Matt, for getting me hooked on Sriracha-drenched fries.* One day, while enjoying them alongside a grapefruit mimosa (read: nursing a hangover), I wondered how they would taste with kimchi. This recipe was born three hours later. Yes, I ate fries twice in one day.

1. In a medium saucepan, melt vegan butter over medium heat. Stir in Sriracha sauce and lemon juice. Increase heat to medium-high and cook for 3 to 5 minutes, whisking constantly, until bubbling. Immediately reduce heat to medium and boil gently, whisking constantly, for 5 to 10 minutes or until slightly thickened and not runny. Transfer to a large bowl and set aside to cool and thicken while you prepare the rest of the recipe.

2. In a small skillet, cook kimchi over medium-high heat, stirring, for 3 minutes, until softened. Remove from the skillet and set aside.

3. Add fries to Sriracha mixture; toss to coat.

4. Transfer fries to a serving dish or four individual plates. Top with kimchi, cilantro and green onions. Sprinkle with sesame seeds and serve immediately.

1/2 cup vegan butter 125 mL
1 cup Sriracha sauce 250 mL
2 tbsp freshly squeezed lemon juice 30 mL
2 cups Fish-Free Kimchi (page 228), chopped 500 mL
1 recipe Potatoes Served in the French Manner (page 224) 1
1 cup fresh cilantro, finely chopped 250 mL
2 green onions, sliced 2
2 tbsp sesame seeds 30 mL

~~ *HACK IT!* ~~

Try this topped with pulled jackfruit (page 199). It's like Korean BBQ heaven.

You can also use store-bought frozen fries to make this recipe even quicker and easier!

Pocket Pizza

MAKES 12 POCKETS

Ah, the pocket pizza. You know it by so many familiar names: the pizza pop, panzerotto, calzone or, for James, "lunch and dinner from high school through university." Let's just call it what it is — a pizza that fits in your pocket. Now, you didn't hear it from me, but it's perfect for smuggling into places that don't offer vegan food: theaters, concerts, your parents' house for Sunday dinner . . .

1. In a small bowl, combine coconut oil and garlic powder. Set aside.

2. Allow dough balls to come to room temperature and set on an unfloured surface. Using a knife, cut each ball into three equal parts to make 12 pieces of dough. One at a time, roll each piece into a ball.

3. Using a rolling pin, roll out each ball of dough into a circle about 1/4 inch (0.5 cm) thick. Spread half of each piece of dough with 1 to 2 spoonfuls of marinara, making sure to leave enough room around the edge to fold and pinch closed. Evenly distribute veggie sausage, green onion, mushrooms, basil, dried oregano and a sprinkle of red pepper flakes; finish with a dollop of cheese. Fold over the opposite side and pinch edges to seal. Press edges with a fork to decorate, and prick the highest part of the pocket to allow steam to escape.

4. Transfer each pocket to a prepared baking sheet, spacing 1 inch (2.5 cm) apart. Brush tops with coconut oil mixture. Bake in preheated oven for 20 to 30 minutes, or until golden brown.

5. Serve with additional marinara or ranch sauce for dipping.

～ HACK IT! ～

Change up the ingredients in your pocket pizzas to create multiple variations of this recipe. My fave combinations are Shredded Hogtown Jackfruit (page 199) and jalapeños; veggie sausage (Hack It! page 41) and pineapple; and veggie pepperoni and green bell pepper.

PREHEAT OVEN TO 375°F
(190°C)
ROLLING PIN
BAKING SHEET LINED WITH
PARCHMENT PAPER

1 tbsp coconut oil, melted 15 mL

1 tsp garlic powder 5 mL

1 recipe Pizzeria-Style Dough (page 31), prepared through Step 3 1

1 recipe Marinara Italiano (page 57) 1

2 veggie sausages, sliced (Hack It! page 41) 2

2 green onions, thinly sliced 2

2 cups sliced cremini mushrooms 500 mL

1/2 cup fresh basil, roughly chopped 125 mL

2 tbsp dried oregano 30 mL

Red pepper flakes, as needed

1 recipe It's a Bella Mozzarella (page 37) 1

1 recipe Ranch Sauce (page 141; optional) 1

Buffalo Cauliflower Wings 7 Ways

SERVES 4

The creation of Buffalo cauliflower wings changed my vegan life forever. They are by far our most popular recipe, both on the blog and in real life. If you want to convert someone from the dark side, this is the dish to make. No one can resist a perfectly breaded and crispy bite of cauliflower slathered in sauce. If I post a photo of these wings, I immediately get texts from five friends announcing that they're "just popping by to say hi." They are that good.

1. In a large bowl, toss cauliflower with olive oil. Spread on a prepared baking sheet and roast in the preheated oven for 40 minutes, flipping halfway, until soft and slightly browned on the edges.

2. Meanwhile, place eggless dip in a large bowl. Set aside.

3. In another large bowl, whisk together flour, rock salt, garlic salt, paprika, garlic powder, onion salt and pepper. Set aside.

4. In a deep fryer or heavy-bottomed saucepan, heat vegetable oil to 350°F (180°C). If you are frying on the stove, you'll need roughly 2 to 3 inches (5 to 7.5 cm) of oil.

5. Toss roasted cauliflower in flour mixture and shake off any excess. Transfer cauliflower to eggless dip and toss to coat. Transfer cauliflower back into flour mixture and toss well to coat.

6. Cook cauliflower in hot oil in batches, a handful at a time, for about 3 to 4 minutes, turning occasionally, until golden brown and crispy. Place fried cauliflower on a tray or bowl lined with paper towel to soak up excess oil. Let oil return to 350°F (180°C) between batches.

7. Toss finished cauliflower in sauce of choice (pages 140 and 141), dip cooked wings into selected sauces, or eat au natural.

PREHEAT OVEN TO 425°F (220°C)
BAKING SHEET LINED WITH PARCHMENT PAPER
DEEP FRYER OR HEAVY-BOTTOMED SAUCE-PAN FITTED WITH A DEEP-FRY THERMOMETER

2 large heads cauliflower, cut into large drumstick-like pieces 2
1 tbsp olive oil 15 mL
1 recipe Eggcellent Eggless Dip (page 35) 1
2 cups unbleached all-purpose flour 500 mL
1 tsp Himalayan rock salt 5 mL
1 tsp garlic salt 5 mL
1 tbsp paprika 15 mL
1 tsp garlic powder 5 mL
1 tsp onion salt 5 mL
1 tsp freshly ground black pepper 5 mL
Vegetable oil for frying

Buffalo Sauce

MAKES ABOUT 1-1/4 CUPS (300 ML)

I love hot sauce, and the only thing better than ordinary hot sauce is velvety homemade Buffalo sauce.

1. In a blender, combine cayenne pepper sauce, vegan butter, vinegar, paprika, vegan Worcestershire, cayenne pepper, garlic powder and sea salt; blend on High until smooth.

2. In a small saucepan, bring hot sauce mixture to a boil over medium heat, whisking constantly. Immediately reduce heat to low and keep warm until ready to use.

BLENDER

2/3 cup cayenne pepper sauce, such as Frank's 150 mL
1/2 cup vegan butter, softened 125 mL
1-1/2 tbsp white vinegar 22 mL
1 tbsp paprika 15 mL
1/4 tsp vegan Worcestershire 1 mL
1/4 tsp cayenne pepper 1 mL
1/8 tsp garlic powder 0.5 mL
Sea salt

Five-Alarm

MAKES ABOUT 1-1/4 CUPS (300 ML)

Regular Buffalo sauce not hot enough for ya? Try this light-your-mouth-on-fire version for brave souls.

1. In a small saucepan, heat Buffalo sauce, cayenne and hot sauce over medium-high heat, whisking constantly, for about 3 minutes, until heated through. Immediately reduce heat to low and keep warm until ready to use.

1 recipe Buffalo Sauce (above) 1
1 tsp cayenne pepper 5 mL
1 tbsp habanero hot sauce 15 mL

Maple Garlic

MAKES ABOUT 3/4 CUP (175 ML)

It's like honey garlic, but Canadian! There is nothing better than the combination of sweet and salty.

1. In a small saucepan, heat vegan butter over medium-high heat. Add garlic and sauté for 1 minute, until fragrant. Add maple syrup, soy sauce and mustard powder; cook, whisking, for 3 minutes, until hot and bubbling. Immediately reduce heat to low and keep warm until ready to use.

2 tbsp vegan butter 30 mL
2 cloves garlic, minced 2
1/2 cup pure maple syrup 125 mL
3 tbsp soy sauce or tamari 45 mL
1 tsp dry mustard powder 5 mL

Jerk Chicken

MAKES ABOUT 1/2 CUP (125 ML)

Get a much-needed vacation with this wing sauce that will make you feel like you're on a hot Caribbean island. It's just the right mix of sweet and earthy, with a hint of spice.

1. In a large bowl, sprinkle wings with garlic, onion and thyme; toss to coat. Add jerk paste; toss to coat cauliflower completely.

1 recipe Buffalo Cauliflower Wings (page 138) 1
1 tsp dried garlic granules 5 mL
1 tsp dried onion flakes 5 mL
1 tsp dried thyme 5 mL
1/2 cup vegan-friendly jerk paste 125 mL

Jalapeño Cheddar

MAKES ABOUT 2 CUPS (500 ML)

This sauce is like a super-spicy cheese sauce. Yup, cheese sauce on wings . . . just try it!

1. In a small saucepan, heat Buffalo sauce, jalapeños and nutritional yeast over medium-high heat for about 3 minutes, stirring constantly, until heated through. Immediately reduce heat to low and keep warm until ready to use.

1 recipe Buffalo Sauce (page 140) 1
1/4 cup pickled jalapeño slices, chopped 60 mL
1/2 cup nutritional yeast 125 mL

Ranch Sauce

MAKES ABOUT 1-1/4 CUPS (300 ML)

Counterbalance all that spice by dunking your wings in this cooling ranch dip.

1. In a blender, combine nutritional yeast, garlic powder, onion powder, pepper, parsley, basil and sea salt; blend on High until a fine powder forms.

2. Transfer to a small mixing bowl. Whisk in dill and cream until smooth. Serve with wings as a dipping sauce.

COFFEE/SPICE GRINDER OR BLENDER

2 tbsp nutritional yeast 30 mL
1 tsp garlic powder 5 mL
1 tbsp onion powder 15 mL
1/4 tsp freshly ground black pepper 1 mL
1 tbsp dried parsley 15 mL
1 tbsp dried basil 15 mL
1/2 tsp sea salt 2 mL
1 tsp finely chopped fresh dill 5 mL
1 cup Essential Non-Dairy Cream (page 49) 250 mL

Scallops in White Wine Butter Sauce

SERVES 4 TO 6 AS AN APPETIZER

If you've got a hot date tonight, this is the appetizer for you. It's an easy and impressive starter that's wildly delicious, and it's light enough not to ruin the main course. Vegan seafood hasn't always been an easy sell with James, so I must say I surprised the both of us when I had Mr. Fancy Frenchman's seal of approval on this one. Scallops: the *other* other white meat.

1. Slice mushroom stems crosswise into 1-inch (2.5 cm) pieces.

2. In a large bowl, whisk together vegetable broth, 1 cup (250 mL) white wine, kelp and 1 tbsp (15 mL) olive oil. Add mushrooms and soak for 1 hour.

3. Preheat oven to 200°F (100°C).

4. Place nutritional yeast in a coffee/spice grinder or blender and pulse until a fine powder forms. Set aside.

5. Drain mushrooms, discarding soaking liquid, and pat dry. In a large skillet, heat 1 tbsp (15 mL) olive oil over medium heat. Add mushrooms and cook for about 6 minutes on each side, until brown. Remove mushrooms from the skillet and keep warm on a plate in preheated oven.

6. Melt 1 tbsp (15 mL) vegan butter in the same skillet over medium heat. Add garlic, shallot, nutritional yeast and tarragon; sauté for about 3 minutes, until soft.

7. Slowly add remaining 1 cup (250 mL) white wine, stirring constantly, and boil for about 5 to 10 minutes, stirring occasionally, until liquid has thickened slightly. Add remaining vegan butter, 1 tbsp (15 mL) at a time, whisking to melt each time before adding the next. When all the butter has melted, taste and season with sea salt and pepper, if necessary.

8. Spoon 2 tbsp (30 mL) white wine sauce onto each plate, arrange a few arugula leaves on top and add 3 seared mushroom scallops. Gently spoon 1 tbsp (15 mL) sauce onto each scallop, sprinkle with truffle salt and garnish with 1 or 2 microgreens, if using.

COFFEE/SPICE GRINDER OR BLENDER

6 large king oyster mushrooms, trimmed and caps removed 6

1-1/2 cups All You Need Is Broth (page 34), hot 375 mL

2 cups dry white wine, divided 500 mL

1-1/2 tsp kelp granules 7 mL

2 tbsp olive oil, divided 30 mL

1 tsp nutritional yeast 5 mL

5 tbsp vegan butter, cold and divided 75 mL

2 cloves garlic, minced 2

1 small shallot, minced 1

1 tsp dried tarragon 5 mL

Sea salt and freshly ground black pepper

Arugula

Truffle salt or coarse sea salt

Microgreens (optional)

A Mezze Named Muhammara

MAKES ROUGHLY 2 CUPS (500 ML)

In the Middle East, you win friends and influence people with dips. Given how much of this stuff we go through in our home, I can tell you, we've got a lot of friends. Swap out your tired hummus for this deep red, sweet and tangy red pepper and walnut dip.

1. Place peppers skin side up on a prepared baking sheet. Place on the top rack of oven and broil for about 10 minutes, until skins are charred.

2. Transfer peppers to a medium bowl, cover with plastic wrap and let cool for 15 minutes. Peel off charred skins and discard.

3. In a food processor, combine green onions and garlic; process until minced. Add roasted peppers, paprika, lemon juice, cumin, sea salt, pomegranate molasses, red pepper flakes, walnuts and bread crumbs; pulse to combine. While pulsing, add olive oil through the feed tube in a steady stream, until just combined. (Pulse for longer if you want the dip to be completely smooth.) Season to taste with sea salt and red pepper flakes. Garnish with additional chopped green onions, if desired.

4. Serve in a small bowl with Lebanese-style pita or use as a sandwich spread. Transfer to a container and store in the fridge for 7 days.

PREHEAT BROILER
BAKING SHEET LINED WITH PARCHMENT PAPER
FOOD PROCESSOR

2 large red bell peppers, halved 2
3 green onions, white and light green parts only, roughly chopped 3
1 garlic clove, crushed 1
1 tsp paprika 5 mL
1 tsp freshly squeezed lemon juice 5 mL
1 tsp ground cumin 5 mL
1/2 tsp sea salt 2 mL
1 tbsp pomegranate molasses 15 mL
1/2 tsp red pepper flakes (approx.) 2 mL
1 cup unsalted walnuts 250 mL
1/4 cup dried bread crumbs 60 mL
3 tbsp olive oil 45 mL
Sea salt
Lebanese-style pita cut into triangles
Additional chopped green onions (optional)

A Terrine to Remember

SERVES 10 AS AN APPETIZER

Let's be frank, terrine does not photograph well. Like a good vintage piece, we don't talk about how it looks on its own or what it took to get there, but paired with the right accessories, it's art. With some artisan (vegan) cheese, baguette crisps and gherkins on a nouveau-vintage platter alongside a decanted bottle of boxed wine, this bougie delicacy will impress even the most elite hipster.

1. In a large bowl, whisk together 2 tbsp (30 mL) olive oil, lemon juice, tamari, rosemary and 1/2 cup (125 mL) vegetable broth. Add oyster mushrooms; toss to coat and let stand for 15 minutes, stirring every 5 minutes, to ensure mushrooms are all coated.

2. In a medium saucepan, heat 1 tbsp (15 mL) olive oil over medium-high heat. Add onion and garlic; sauté for about 3 minutes, until translucent. Add portobello mushrooms and sun-dried tomatoes and bring to a boil. Immediately reduce heat to medium and simmer for 15 minutes, stirring occasionally, or until tomatoes and mushrooms are tender. Transfer to a large bowl and set aside.

3. Heat the same medium saucepan over medium-high heat. Drain oyster mushrooms, discarding liquid, and add to the pan. Sauté mushrooms for 5 to 10 minutes, stirring constantly, until soft. Remove from heat and set aside.

4. Preheat oven to 350°F (180°C).

5. In a food processor, combine sunflower seeds, potato starch, Vegemite, nutritional yeast, liquid smoke, sea salt and pepper; process until a coarse paste forms. (It will take longer than you think). Taste and add more sea salt and pepper, if necessary.

6. Transfer portobello mixture to the food processor; pulse to combine. Add carrots, parsley and oyster mushrooms; pulse just to combine. You want some texture in this terrine, so do not overprocess.

7. Spread mixture into a prepared loaf pan and cover with foil. Bake in the preheated oven for 1 hour, until firm.

8. Remove from oven, place on a wire rack and remove foil. Let cool for 1 hour, then cover with plastic wrap and transfer to the fridge for a minimum of 8 hours or up to 3 days.

8- BY 4-INCH (20 BY 10 CM) LOAF PAN LINED WITH CRISSCROSSED PIECES OF PARCHMENT PAPER
FOOD PROCESSOR

3 tbsp olive oil, divided 45 mL
1-1/2 tsp freshly squeezed lemon juice 7 mL
2 tbsp tamari 30 mL
1/2 tsp dried rosemary 2 mL
1 cup All You Need Is Broth (page 34), divided 250 mL
2 cups sliced king oyster mushrooms 500 mL
1 small onion, chopped 1
1 garlic clove, minced 1
4 cups sliced portobello mushrooms 1 L
2 oil-packed sun-dried tomatoes, drained and chopped 2
1 cup raw sunflower seeds 250 mL
1 tbsp potato starch 15 mL
1 tsp Vegemite 5 mL
1 tbsp nutritional yeast 15 mL
1/4 tsp liquid smoke 1 mL
1 tsp sea salt (approx.) 5 mL
1/4 tsp freshly ground black pepper (approx.) 1 mL
2 carrots, chopped 2
1/4 cup fresh curly parsley, chopped 60 mL

9. To serve, carefully invert the terrine onto a serving dish and carefully remove parchment paper. Cut into slices and serve.

∼ HACK IT! ∼

This terrine can be refrigerated for 3 days, making this a bomb make-ahead recipe.

Mason-Dixon Crab Melt

SERVES 4

Veganizing seafood can leave me feeling a bit crabby. I feel like I'm constantly taking two steps sideways and one step back. Did you sea what I did there? I'm shore you did. This dip is perfect to have around in a *pinch* for parties. It's rich, creamy and indulgent, with a crispy, buttery topping that you won't be able to keep your fingers or bread products out of.

1. In a large bowl, combine hearts of palm, 2 tbsp (30 mL) olive oil, Old Bay seasoning and garlic. Let stand for at least 1 hour, but overnight is best.

2. Preheat oven to 425°F (220°C).

3. In a medium skillet over medium-high heat, cook hearts of palm along with the marinade, stirring occasionally, for 8 minutes, until slightly brown. Remove from the pan, place in a large bowl and set aside to cool.

4. In the same skillet, heat 1 tbsp (15 mL) olive oil over medium-high heat. Add green onions and red pepper; sauté for about 5 minutes, until soft. Remove from heat.

5. In a food processor, combine green onion mixture, fondue cheese, sour cream, mayo, lemon juice, paprika, chives, dill and sea salt; process until creamy. (You can also mix with a fork if you don't own a food processor.)

6. Using a spatula, gently fold cheese mixture into hearts of palm until combined. Spread mixture evenly into a prepared baking dish.

7. In a small bowl, combine panko, nutritional yeast and melted vegan butter; sprinkle over baking dish.

8. Bake in preheated oven for 20 to 30 minutes, until bread crumbs have turned golden brown and "cheese" is bubbling. Remove from heat and serve with a sprinkling of chopped chives, chopped dill and paprika.

HACK IT!

Make this recipe gluten-free by simply omitting the panko crumbs and serving with your favorite gluten-free cracker or fresh cut veggies.

8-INCH (20 CM) SQUARE GLASS OR OVAL CERAMIC BAKING DISH, LIGHTLY GREASED
FOOD PROCESSOR (OPTIONAL)

1 can (14 oz /398 mL) hearts of palm in water, drained, rinsed, dried and roughly chopped to resemble crab meat 1

3 tbsp olive oil, divided 45 mL

1 tbsp Old Bay seasoning 15 mL

1 garlic clove, minced 1

3 green onions, white and light green parts only, minced 3

1/2 small red bell pepper, finely chopped 1/2

1 cup Fondue Cheese (page 178) 250 mL

1/3 cup Burrito-Worthy Sour Cream (page 51) 75 mL

1/3 cup Hell No! Egg-Free Mayo (page 50) 75 mL

1 tsp freshly squeezed lemon juice 5 mL

1/2 tsp sweet paprika 2 mL

2 tbsp minced fresh chives 30 mL

2 tsp minced fresh dill 10 mL

1/4 tsp sea salt 1 mL

1 cup panko bread crumbs 250 mL

1/4 cup nutritional yeast 60 mL

3 tbsp vegan butter, melted 45 mL

Chopped chives

Chopped dill (optional)

Sweet paprika

Austin-Tacious Roasted Salsa

SERVES 4 TO 6

James rates every Mexican restaurant on the quality of its salsa — tacos and burritos are just the accoutrements. The full-bodied flavor of this stuff will make you never want to buy anything from the store again. Serve warm with tortilla chips alongside our Loaded Breakfast Burritos (page 69), Naked Burrito (page 102) or Crunchy Taco Wrap Supreme (page 204).

PREHEAT BROILER
FOOD PROCESSOR OR BLENDER

10 Roma tomatoes, halved lengthwise 10
2 jalapeño peppers, halved 2
1 large white onion, halved and sliced 1/2 inch (1 cm) thick 1
6 garlic cloves, unpeeled 6
3 tbsp olive oil 45 mL
1/2 cup fresh cilantro 125 mL
1 tbsp freshly squeezed lime juice 15 mL
1-1/4 tsp sea salt 6 mL
1/4 tsp ground cumin 1 mL
1 tsp organic sugar 5 mL
Tortilla chips

1. In a large bowl, combine tomatoes, jalapeños, onion, garlic and olive oil; toss to coat.

2. Spread vegetables on a baking sheet, ensuring that tomatoes and jalapeños are skin side up. Place on the top rack of oven and broil for 7 minutes or until skins of tomatoes and jalapeños have blackened thoroughly and are beginning to peel. With a pair of tongs, flip veggies and cook for another 5 minutes, or until vegetables are cooked through.

3. Remove from oven and let cool for 15 minutes. Remove peel from garlic cloves.

4. In a food processor, combine roasted vegetables (including all those wonderful juices) and cilantro; process until salsa is smooth but a little chunky (or leave it chunky, if you like it that way). Add lime juice, sea salt, cumin and sugar, and pulse to combine. Adjust lime juice and sea salt to taste. Serve warm with tortilla chips.

 HACK IT!

Turn down the heat by discarding the seeds in your jalapeño peppers.

For extra hipster bonus points, you can refrigerate the salsa in a mason jar for up to 3 days.

The Main Squeeze

/mān skwēz/ *noun*

1. A person's foremost girlfriend, boyfriend, sweetheart or lover • *"Victor, I'd like you to meet Heather, my main squeeze."*
2. The primary romantic partner, in among other, less important side partners. *"I spent Friday with Todd, but I'm looking forward to hanging out with my main squeeze, Joshua, tomorrow afternoon."*
3. The most substantial course in a meal; the highlight of a culinary experience.

THIS CHAPTER IS WHAT YOU CAME FOR. Sides are important, but let's be honest, their main purpose is to highlight the *plat principal*. Nothing is going to satisfy you like a plate of In Search of General Tso's Chicken, Famous Edgy Veg Fried Chicken or Steaks with Béarnaise Sauce. Hell, they might even get you a second date with Todd OR Joshua.

Perfectly Pleasing Pesto Pizza

MAKES 4 PIZZAS (SERVES 6 TO 8)

This recipe was inspired by one of the best pizzas I've ever had — and I've had A LOT of pizza. The nuttiness of the pesto, the sweet roasted garlic, the acidity of perfectly roasted tomatoes, all held together with a drizzle of sweet agave . . . I just can't quit this flavor combo. James would prefer to have more variety in our at-home pizza, but this isn't about James — this is about me and MY LOVE FOR THIS PIZZA!

1. **Caramelized Onions:** In a large skillet, melt coconut oil over medium heat. Add onions and stir to coat with oil; sauté for 3 minutes, stirring occasionally, until translucent. Reduce heat to medium-low and cook for 45 minutes, stirring every 10 minutes, until onions turn deep brown and are caramelized.

2. Pour wine into skillet and simmer for 1 to 3 minutes, scraping the skillet and stirring onions until liquid has evaporated. Set aside.

3. **Roasted Tomatoes:** In a medium bowl, combine tomatoes, olive oil, fennel seeds, sea salt and pepper. Set aside.

4. **Roasted Garlic:** Peel off the outer layer of each garlic bulb, leaving skins on individual garlic cloves. Cut 1/4 inch (0.5 cm) off the top of garlic bulb, just to expose the flesh. Place each bulb on a square of aluminum foil and drizzle with 1 tsp (5 mL) olive oil. Wrap foil around bulb and place on baking sheet. Place tomatoes, cut side up, on the same baking sheet. Bake garlic for 35 to 40 minutes, or until cloves are soft. Bake tomatoes for 40 minutes, until soft and slightly deflated.

5. Remove tomatoes and garlic from oven and set aside to cool. Once garlic is cool enough to handle, using your fingers, pull roasted cloves out of skins. Slice each clove into quarters and set aside.

6. **Roasted Red Peppers:** Move oven rack to the top of your oven; preheat to Broil. Place peppers, skin side up, on prepared baking sheet; broil for about 10 minutes, until skins are charred.

PREHEAT OVEN TO 300°F (150°C)
2 RIMMED BAKING SHEETS LINED WITH PARCHMENT PAPER
PIPING BAG WITH A LARGE TIP (OPTIONAL)
PIZZA STONE
PIZZA CUTTER (OPTIONAL)

CARAMELIZED ONIONS
2 tbsp coconut oil 30 mL
2 red onions, sliced into 1/8-inch (3 mm) thick half-moons 2
1/4 cup white wine 60 mL

ROASTED TOMATOES
2 cups grape tomatoes, halved 500 mL
1 tbsp olive oil 15 mL
1/2 tsp fennel seeds 2 mL
1/4 tsp sea salt 1 mL
1/4 tsp freshly ground black pepper 1 mL

ROASTED GARLIC
2 garlic bulbs 2
2 tsp olive oil 10 mL

ROASTED RED PEPPERS
2 small red bell peppers, cut in half lengthwise 2

7. Remove from oven and place peppers in a medium bowl. Cover with plastic wrap and let cool for 15 minutes. Peel off the charred skins and discard. Slice peppers lengthwise into thin strips. Set aside.

8. **Assembly:** Preheat a pizza stone in oven set to 500°F (260°C). Spread one crust with 3 to 4 tbsp (45 to 60 mL) pesto, leaving a 1/4-inch (0.5 cm) border. Pipe (or place with a small spoon) dollops of cheese randomly around the pizza. Sprinkle tomatoes, red peppers, onions and garlic overtop.

9. Bake for 6 to 10 minutes, until browned on top and crispy on bottom, and cheese is melted, bubbling and golden brown, but not burned. Repeat with remaining pizzas.

10. Remove from oven and drizzle each pizza with about 1 tbsp (15 mL) agave nectar. Using a pizza cutter or a sharp knife, slice pizzas.

~~ *HACK IT!* ~~

Don't want to make your own cheese or are short on time? Cool! Just use your favorite store-bought vegan mozzarella.

If you don't have a pizza stone, use a round baking sheet and cook for 8 to 12 minutes.

You have 2 minutes to dress your pizza after the sauce has touched the crust to get that sucker in the oven, or else you will have a soggy, sad pizza on your hands. To avoid this, prepare all your toppings in advance and have them in bowls ready for pizza dressing.

1 recipe Pizzeria-Style Dough (page 31), prepared through Step 6 1
1 recipe Presto, Pesto (page 54) 1
1 recipe It's a Bella Mozzarella (page 37) 1
1/4 cup agave nectar 60 mL

Why So Syrian Chicken and Rice

SERVES 5

James is half Syrian, and over the course of our relationship he has taught me that Arabic food isn't all hummus, falafel and baba ghanoush (although I think I could live happily only eating those three dishes). Syrian cuisine is very much built around a rich and welcoming sentiment, like this go-to crowd-pleaser that we often eat for James's family dinners. They call it "the pile," and what a fantastic pile of aromatic seasoned rice, spiced "chicken" and toasted nuts it is!

1. **Rice:** Using a fine-mesh sieve, rinse rice under cold water until water runs clear. In a medium saucepan, combine rice, water, bouillon, bay leaf and a pinch of sea salt; bring to a boil over high heat, stirring to dissolve bouillon cube. Immediately reduce heat to low and cover with a tight-fitting lid. Simmer for 15 minutes, until soft and all the liquid has been absorbed. Remove from heat, cover and set aside. Use a fork to fluff up rice when ready to serve.

2. **Syrian Chicken**: Meanwhile, in a small bowl, whisk together cornstarch and 3 tbsp (45 mL) water. Set aside.

3. In a large skillet, heat 2 tbsp (30 mL) olive oil over medium-high heat. Add onion and garlic; sauté for 3 to 5 minutes, until translucent. Add saffron, marjoram and allspice; sauté, for about 1 minute, until fragrant. Add veggie ground round and 2 tbsp (30 mL) water; sauté for about 10 minutes, until heated through. Set aside.

4. Meanwhile, in a medium skillet, heat 2 tbsp (30 mL) olive oil over medium-high heat. Add curry powder, cinnamon and herbes de Provence; sauté for about 1 minute, until fragrant. Be careful not to burn the herbs. Add 1 cup (250 mL) water and 1/2 bouillon cube and cook for about 3 minutes, until bouillon cube is dissolved and mixture is heated through. Add seitan; simmer, stirring often, for about 10 minutes, until liquid has reduced by one-third. Season with sea salt to taste.

5. Using a slotted spoon, transfer seitan to a large bowl, leaving liquid in the pan. Taste broth in the skillet and adjust sea salt and pepper to taste. Turn up heat to high and cook for another 5 minutes, until reduced by one-quarter. Add cornstarch mixture; whisk until thickened and smooth and resembles gravy. Immediately remove from heat.

FINE-MESH SIEVE

RICE
1 cup white rice 250 mL
2 cups water 500 mL
1 vegetable bouillon cube 1
1 bay leaf 1
Sea salt

SYRIAN CHICKEN
1 tbsp cornstarch 15 mL
1-1/3 cups water, divided 325 mL
1/3 cup olive oil, divided 75 mL
1 onion, diced 1
2 garlic cloves, minced 2
2 freshly ground saffron threads 2
1/2 tsp dried marjoram 2 mL
1 tsp ground allspice 5 mL
12 oz veggie ground round or texturized vegetable protein 375 g
1 tbsp curry powder 15 mL
1/4 tsp ground cinnamon 1 mL
1 tbsp herbes de Provence 15 mL
1/2 vegetable bouillon cube 1/2
1-1/2 cups diced Become a Master of Seitan: Chicken (Breasts, page 39) 375 mL
Sea salt and freshly ground black pepper
1/4 cup pine nuts 60 mL
1/4 cup finely chopped curly parsley 60 mL
Plain vegan yogurt (optional)

6. In a small skillet, heat 1 tbsp (15 mL) olive oil over medium heat. Add pine nuts and toast, stirring constantly, for 1 to 2 minutes, until golden brown. This will happen quickly, so pay attention. Transfer to a small bowl and set aside.

7. Add cooked rice to seitan; toss well to combine. Transfer rice mixture to a large serving dish or bowl and top with ground round, half the parsley and half the pine nuts. Toss gently, just to combine. Garnish with the remaining pine nuts and parsley, and serve with gravy and plain vegan yogurt, if desired.

HACK IT!

You can use any store-bought chicken substitute for the seitan.

This recipe is the perfect family-style meal. Let everyone serve themselves rice and a side of yogurt and then pass around the coveted gravy.

In Search of General Tso's Chicken

SERVES 4

It's no wonder this is North America's most popular "Chinese" dish. What's not to love? It's the perfect balance of sweet, salty and spicy, not to mention that it's deep-fried and covered in sauce. As far as I'm concerned, it doesn't matter if you're a Qing dynasty military leader or a Taiwan-based Hunan chef, this dish has everything you need to be happy in life.

1. In large bowl, combine cauliflower with 1 tbsp (15 mL) vegetable oil; toss to coat. Transfer to a prepared baking sheet. Roast in the preheated oven for 25 minutes, flipping after 15 minutes, until soft and golden brown. Set aside to cool for 10 minutes.

2. In a medium saucepan, bring 2 cups (500 mL) water to a boil over high heat. Add rice and immediately reduce heat to low. Cover with a tight-fitting lid and simmer for 15 minutes, until soft and all the liquid has been absorbed. Remove from heat and let stand, covered, while you prepare the rest of the recipe. Use a fork to fluff up rice when ready to serve.

3. In a deep fryer or heavy-bottomed saucepan, heat vegetable oil to between 350°F (180°C) and 375°F (190°C). If you are frying on the stove, you'll need at least 3 inches (7.5 cm) of oil.

4. While oil is heating up, in a small bowl, whisk together soy sauce, rice vinegar, hoisin sauce, 1/2 cup (125 mL) water, maple syrup, wine, lime juice and 1 tbsp (15 mL) cornstarch. Set aside.

5. In a medium bowl, whisk together remaining 2/3 cup (150 mL) cornstarch and sea salt. Add roasted cauliflower and toss to coat.

6. In batches, fry cauliflower in hot oil for about 4 minutes, until the pieces turn light brown and crispy. Remove cauliflower with a slotted spoon, draining excess oil, and lay on a plate lined with paper towel.

PREHEAT OVEN TO 450°F (230°C)
BAKING SHEET LINED WITH PARCHMENT PAPER
DEEP FRYER OR HEAVY-BOTTOMED SAUCE-PAN FITTED WITH A DEEP-FRY THERMOMETER
WOK OR LARGE SKILLET

---

1 small head cauliflower, cut into florets 1
Vegetable oil
1 cup white rice, rinsed 250 mL
2-1/2 cups water, divided 625 mL
Vegetable oil for frying
1/4 cup soy sauce or tamari 60 mL
1/4 cup seasoned rice vinegar 60 mL
3 tbsp hoisin sauce 45 mL
2 tbsp pure maple syrup 30 mL
1 tbsp Shaoxing wine 15 mL
1 tbsp freshly squeezed lime juice 15 mL
2/3 cup + 1 tbsp cornstarch, divided 165 mL
1/2 tsp sea salt 2 mL
1 1-inch (2.5 cm) piece fresh ginger, finely minced 1
1 garlic clove, minced 1
4 dried red chiles, seeded 4
4 green onions, cut into 1-inch (2.5 cm) pieces 4
Sesame seeds

7. In a large wok, heat 1-1/2 tbsp (22 mL) vegetable oil over medium heat. Add ginger, garlic and chiles; stir-fry for about 1 to 2 minutes, until fragrant. Add soy sauce mixture and cook, whisking constantly, for 3 minutes, until sauce begins to boil and thicken slightly. Add fried cauliflower and stir to coat. Add green onions and stir a few times to coat. Garnish with sesame seeds and serve over a bed of rice.

HACK IT!

Shaoxing wine can be found in most Asian grocery stores. If you have trouble finding it, you can use dry sherry instead.

Gnocchi Puttanesca!

SERVES 4

I once read that Neapolitan courtesans would lure men from the street with the intense aroma of their pasta alla puttanesca. So, if you're trying to get to your man's heart through his stomach, I can guarantee your guy will fall hard with this one. Fun fact: The literal translation of *gnocchi puttanesca* is "gnocchi in the style of a prostitute." Take that as you will, *bella*.

1. In a large saucepan, heat olive oil over medium heat. Add garlic and red pepper flakes; sauté for about 3 to 4 minutes, until garlic is fragrant and golden. Stir in capers, olives and nutritional yeast; sauté for 1 minute, until fragrant. Add tomatoes and bring to a simmer, stirring occasionally, over medium-high heat. Reduce heat to medium-low and simmer, stirring occasionally, for 20 minutes, until reduced slightly. Taste and season with sea salt and pepper, if desired.

2. Add gnocchi to sauce. Gently stir and shake the pan to coat gnocchi in sauce. Add parsley and stir to combine. Transfer to four serving plates. Garnish with additional parsley, black olives and vegan Parmesan, if desired.

HACK IT!

Make this recipe super quick by buying premade gnocchi from the pasta aisle at the supermarket.

1/4 **cup** olive oil 60 mL

4 **garlic** cloves, minced 4

1/2 **tsp** red pepper flakes 2 mL

1/4 **cup** chopped drained capers 60 mL

1/2 **cup** chopped pitted black olives 125 mL

1-1/2 **tbsp** nutritional yeast 22 mL

1 **can** (14 oz/398 mL) crushed tomatoes 1

Sea salt and freshly ground black pepper

1 **recipe** Foolproof Gnocchi (page 32), cooked 1

1/4 **cup** chopped fresh flat-leaf (Italian) parsley 60 mL

Additional chopped fresh flat-leaf (Italian) parsley

Additional chopped pitted black olives

Vegan Parmesan (optional)

Spaghetti and Neat Balls, Bro

SERVES 4

Don't get saucy with me. Low-carb spaghetti?! Sounds like an impasta! Comfort food must be done correctly, and nothing says comfort like good ol'-fashioned, family-friendly, eat-your-feelings spaghetti and neat balls.

1. Bring a large pot of salted water to a boil. Cook spaghetti according to package instructions. Drain.

2. In the pot, toss spaghetti with marinara sauce. Divide evenly between four plates and top with 4 neat balls or more . . . I'm not here to judge your level of ball hunger. Sprinkle with nutritional yeast, pepper and basil, if using. Now enjoy those carbs!

10 oz spaghetti 300 g
1 recipe Marinara Italiano (page 57), warmed 1
1 recipe Neat Balls, Bro (page 44) 1
1/4 cup nutritional yeast or vegan Parmesan 60 mL
1/4 tsp freshly ground black pepper 1 mL
Fresh chopped basil (optional)

Drunken Fish and Chips

SERVES 4

Crispy battered fish and golden chips go together like peanut butter and jam, milk and cookies, anger and veganism. Just kidding — we're not all angry. This dish combines my two favorite things: beer and pub-style food. FYI: eggplant-acting-as-fish isn't all mouth and no trousers. It's just as flaky on the inside and crispy on the outside as the battered fish you'd find at your local London chippy.

1. **Tartar Sauce:** In a small bowl, whisk together mayo, relish, onion and lemon juice. Season to taste with sea salt. Refrigerate while you prepare the rest of the recipe.

2. **Beer-Battered Fish:** In a baking dish, whisk together 1 tbsp (15 mL) kelp granules, lemon juice, garlic powder, wine and vegetable broth. Add eggplant slices and soak, completely covered, in the fridge for a minimum of 2 hours or up to 24 hours, turning once.

3. Using a fork or tongs, remove eggplant from marinade, reserving marinade, and drain on a baking sheet lined with paper towel. Pat eggplant dry with paper towel. Using a pastry brush, dampen each piece of nori with a bit of reserved marinade and place on top of each piece of eggplant. Brush with additional marinade if nori does not stick right away. If you have more than 6 slices, use more nori to cover the extras. Set aside.

4. Preheat oven to 225°F (110°C).

5. In a deep fryer or heavy-bottomed saucepan, heat vegetable oil to 365°F (185°C). If you are frying on the stove, you'll need at least 3 inches (7.5 cm) of oil.

6. In a large bowl, whisk together flour, egg replacer, baking powder, Old Bay, remaining 1 tsp (5 mL) kelp, pepper, sea salt and garlic powder. Carefully pour in beer, whisking gently, until a smooth, thick batter forms. Drink any beer that is left over.

7. One at a time, swirl eggplant slices around in batter until well coated. Immediately add to hot oil. Fry in hot oil for 4 to 5 minutes, until batter becomes crisp and golden brown. Using tongs, remove eggplant, gently shaking off

9-INCH (23 CM) SQUARE GLASS BAKING DISH
DEEP FRYER OR HEAVY-BOTTOMED SAUCE-PAN FITTED WITH A DEEP-FRY THERMOMETER

TARTAR SAUCE
1/2 cup Hell No! Egg-Free Mayo (page 50) 125 mL
3 tbsp sweet green relish 45 mL
1-1/2 tsp minced onion 7 mL
1 tbsp freshly squeezed lemon juice 15 mL
Sea salt

BEER-BATTERED FISH
4 tsp kelp granules, divided 20 mL
1 tbsp freshly squeezed lemon juice 15 mL
1 tsp garlic powder 5 mL
1 cup dry white wine 250 mL
1 cup All You Need Is Broth (page 34) 250 mL
1 large long eggplant, cut lengthwise into 6 1/2-inch (1 cm) slices 1
3 8-inch (20 cm) nori sheets, halved 3
Vegetable oil for frying
1-1/2 cups unbleached all-purpose flour 375 mL
1 tbsp egg replacer powder (I like Ener-G) 15 mL

excess oil, and place on a plate lined with paper towel. Keep warm in the preheated oven until ready to serve. Fry the remaining eggplant slices in batches, returning oil to 365°F (185°C) between batches. Discard any excess batter.

8. Raise oil temperature to 375°F (190°C). Fry potatoes in batches, for about 2 minutes, until golden brown. Using tongs, remove potatoes, gently shaking off excess oil, and place in a mixing bowl lined with paper towel. Sprinkle with paprika, sea salt and pepper, adding more to taste, if desired, and toss to coat.

9. Serve 1 to 2 pieces of eggplant per person with french fries, malt vinegar, if desired, and a side of tartar sauce. Don't forget to drink a pint of warm beer and throw *Coronation Street* on the telly!

2 tbsp baking powder 30 mL
1-1/2 tsp Old Bay seasoning 7 mL
1/4 tsp freshly ground black pepper 1 mL
1 tsp sea salt 5 mL
1 tsp garlic powder 5 mL
1 cup beer, preferably mild-flavored 250 mL
Paprika
Sea salt and freshly ground black pepper

1 recipe Potatoes Served in the French Manner (page 224), prepared through Step 3 1
Malt vinegar (optional)

HACK IT!

Try seasoning fries with Old Bay seasoning if you want to change it up. It's tasty!

Half-Baked Mac and Cheese

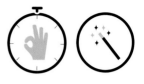

SERVES 4 TO 6

Everyone needs a creamy, ooey-gooey mac-and-cheese recipe in their back pocket. It's the all-purpose comfort food, easily whipped up to assist with any life event. Nothing says "I'm sorry you didn't get that promotion" or "He's such a jerk; you don't need him" like dreamy cheese sauce and pasta, baked in a casserole dish until golden and bubbly.

1. In a large bowl, whisk together cheese sauce and pepper. Set aside.

2. Bring a large pot of salted water to a boil. Cook macaroni for 2 minutes less than package instructions. Drain pasta and transfer back to the pot. Add softened vegan butter and toss until butter is melted and pasta is evenly coated. Add cheese sauce and toss to coat. Season to taste with sea salt and pepper.

3. Pour pasta into baking dish and spread out evenly.

4. In a large bowl, combine melted vegan butter and bread crumbs. Sprinkle breadcrumb mixture over mac and cheese in an even layer. Bake for about 30 minutes, until crust is browned and bubbling. Remove from the oven and serve immediately.

PREHEAT OVEN TO 400°F (200°C)
13- BY 9-INCH (33 BY 23 CM) BAKING DISH

1 recipe The Art of Cheese Sauce (page 52) 1
1/4 tsp freshly ground black pepper 1 mL
1 lb macaroni 500 g
2 tbsp softened vegan butter 30 mL
Sea salt
3 tbsp melted vegan butter 45 mL
1 cup panko bread crumbs 250 mL

HACK IT!

Truffle this mac and cheese by combining the hot pasta with 1 tbsp (15 mL) truffle oil before adding the cheese sauce.

James likes it spicy, so I often add 2 chopped jalapeño peppers and 1 tsp (5 mL) Tabasco sauce to the cheese sauce, to accommodate his need for fire.

Make this recipe gluten-free by using your favorite gluten-free pasta, like brown rice or corn, and omitting the breadcrumb topping.

Italian Bakery Veal Parmigiana

SERVES 6

Yes, I am aware that veal Parmesan is about as Italian as Olive Garden. Nonetheless, this is the perfect Sunday night dinner. Not only does it provide a good-for-the-whole-family type of comfort, it's also a pleasure to prepare. I like to serve it with The Buffalo Caesar (page 105), spaghetti and marinara sauce or crusty bread.

1. In a deep fryer or heavy-bottomed saucepan, heat vegetable oil to between 350°F (180°C) and 375°F (190°C). If you are frying on the stove, you will need at least 3 inches (7.5 cm) of oil.

2. Prepare three wide, shallow bowls for dipping. In the first, whisk together 1 cup (250 mL) flour and black pepper; place eggless dip in the second bowl; and in the third, whisk together bread crumbs and 1 tbsp (15 mL) flour. Dip a piece of cooked schnitzel in flour, then into eggless dip and finally coat completely with bread crumbs. Place on a prepared baking sheet and repeat with the remaining schnitzels.

3. One at a time, fry a schnitzel in hot oil, for about 1-1/2 minutes on each side, until crispy and golden. Using tongs, remove from oil, shake off excess oil and place on a baking sheet or a plate lined with paper towel. Blot excess oil with paper towel. Repeat with the remaining schnitzels.

4. Place all cutlets, side by side, on the second prepared baking pan. Top each cutlet with a slice of vegan cheese and 1/2 cup (125 mL) marinara sauce, leaving the edges exposed for a nice crispy crust. Top with a second layer of cheese.

5. Bake in the preheated oven for 20 minutes, until cheese is melted. Garnish with fresh basil and parsley; serve.

HACK IT!

Toss these prepared schnitzels (baked with sauce and cheese) on a Kaiser bun, along with some roasted bell peppers and roasted mushrooms (page 216), and you've got yourself an Italian veal sandwich panino — *bene!*

PREHEAT OVEN TO 400°F (200°C)

DEEP FRYER OR HEAVY-BOTTOMED SAUCE-PAN FITTED WITH A DEEP-FRY THERMOMETER

2 BAKING SHEETS LINED WITH PARCHMENT PAPER

Vegetable oil for frying

1 cup + **1 tbsp** unbleached all-purpose flour, divided 265 mL

1 tsp freshly ground black pepper 5 mL

1 recipe Eggcellent Eggless Dip (page 35) 1

2 cups dried bread crumbs 500 mL

Become a Master of Seitan: Chicken (Schnitzels, page 39)

12 slices It's a Bella Mozzarella (page 37) or vegan cheese of choice 12

1 recipe Marinara Italiano (page 57) 1

1/4 cup fresh basil, chopped 60 mL

1/4 cup fresh flat-leaf (Italian) parsley, chopped 60 mL

Famous Edgy Veg Fried Chicken

SERVES 6

This is *the* homegrown, Deep South, finger-lickin' good, tried-and-true vegan fried chicken recipe. The first time I made this, I actually cried. Not a single-tear type of cry, but life-is-worth-living-again, blubbering-mess sobs. It's so good, I'll eat the crumbs off the oil-soaked paper towel and not even be ashamed.

1. Divide seitan dough into chicken thigh-, drumstick-, wing- and/or breast-size pieces. Keep in mind that they will grow to about twice their size, so make them a bit smaller than you need them to be.

2. Cook seitan as directed in the chicken burgers recipe (page 38) and place on a wire rack to dry and cool.

3. Place eggless dip in a large bowl. Set aside.

4. In a deep fryer or heavy-bottomed saucepan, heat peanut or vegetable oil to 375°F (190°C). If you are frying on the stove, you'll need at least 3 inches (7.5 cm) of oil.

5. In another large bowl, whisk together flour, poultry seasoning, mustard powder, paprika, garlic powder, sea salt, chili powder, pepper, onion powder and sugar.

6. Add seitan pieces to flour mixture and toss to coat, shaking off any excess flour. Dredge seitan pieces in eggless dip and toss to coat. Place seitan pieces back in flour mixture and toss to coat.

7. In batches, fry seitan in hot oil for 3 to 4 minutes, turning once, until golden brown and crispy. Using a slotted spoon, remove from oil, gently shaking off excess oil, and place on a plate lined with paper towels. Let oil return to 375°F (190°C) between batches.

8. Serve with hot sauce, BBQ sauce, Buffalo Sauce (page 140) or Ranch Sauce (page 141) for dipping.

DEEP FRYER OR HEAVY-BOTTOMED SAUCE-PAN FITTED WITH A DEEP-FRY THERMOMETER

1 recipe Become a Master of Seitan: Chicken (page 38) 1

1 recipe Eggcellent Eggless Dip (page 35) 1

Vegetable oil for frying

2 cups unbleached all-purpose flour 500 mL

1 tbsp poultry seasoning 15 mL

1 tsp dry mustard powder 5 mL

1 tsp paprika 5 mL

1 tsp garlic powder 5 mL

1 tsp sea salt 5 mL

1/2 tsp chili powder 2 mL

1/2 tsp freshly ground black pepper 2 mL

1/2 tsp onion powder 2 mL

1/4 tsp sugar 1 mL

Hot sauce (optional)

Vegan-friendly BBQ sauce (optional)

Buffalo Sauce (page 140; optional)

Ranch Sauce (page 141; optional)

Baja Fish Tacos

SERVES 4

What I love about this recipe is that it's just so easy. It's trendy enough to impress guests, but super easy to whip up after work. You can prep almost everything ahead, and all the ingredients are easy to find. Stop rolling your eyes — you can find kelp in the international section of most grocery stores . . .

1. **Mango Slaw:** In a small bowl, combine mango, cabbage, onion, lime juice, cilantro, sea salt and jalapeño. Set aside.

2. In a deep fryer or heavy-bottomed saucepan, heat vegetable oil to 375°F (190°C). If you are frying on the stove, you'll need at least 3 inches (7.5 cm) of oil.

3. **Tacos:** In another small bowl, whisk together sour cream and lime juice. Voilà! Lime crema! Set aside.

4. Place eggless dip in a medium bowl. Set aside.

5. In another medium bowl, whisk together all-purpose flour, kelp granules, garlic powder, onion powder, paprika, pepper and sea salt. Set aside.

6. Add mushrooms to flour mixture and toss to coat, shaking off any excess flour. Add mushrooms to eggless dip and toss to coat. Place mushrooms back into flour mixture and toss to coat.

7. In batches, fry mushrooms in hot oil for 3 to 5 minutes, turning once if cooking on a stove, until golden brown. Using a slotted spoon, remove mushrooms from oil, shake off excess oil and place on a plate lined with paper towels. Let oil return to 375°F (190°C) between batches.

8. In a large, dry skillet, warm 3 tortillas at a time over medium-low heat, flipping once, for about 30 seconds to 1 minute (or wrap all the tortillas in a damp cloth and microwave for 25 seconds). Wrap in a tea towel to keep warm.

9. Evenly divide mango slaw and breaded mushrooms between tortillas and drizzle with lime crema. Serve 3 tacos to a plate with a lime wedge and an ice-cold Mexican cerveza.

DEEP FRYER OR HEAVY-BOTTOMED SAUCEPAN FITTED WITH A DEEP-FRY THERMOMETER

MANGO SLAW

1 cup finely chopped mango 250 mL

1/2 cup shredded red cabbage 125 mL

1/2 red onion, finely chopped 1/2

1 tbsp freshly squeezed lime juice 15 mL

1/4 cup fresh cilantro, chopped 60 mL

1/8 tsp sea salt 0.5 mL

1 jalapeño pepper, minced 1

TACOS

1/2 cup Burrito-Worthy Sour Cream (page 51) 125 mL

1 tbsp freshly squeezed lime juice 15 mL

1 recipe Eggcellent Eggless Dip (page 35) 1

1 cup unbleached all-purpose flour 250 mL

2 tbsp kelp granules 30 mL

1 tsp garlic powder 5 mL

1/2 tsp onion powder 2 mL

1/2 tsp paprika 2 mL

1 tsp freshly ground black pepper 5 mL

1/2 tsp sea salt 2 mL

3 cups sliced whole oyster mushrooms or portobello mushroom caps 750 mL

Vegetable oil for frying

12 corn tortillas 12

1 lime, cut into wedges 1

Easy Cheesy Fondue

SERVES 4 TO 6

Fondue: the European version of a cheese-eating contest. Whoever decided to make an entire meal out of a bowl of melted cheese is my hero. As a recovering cheese addict myself, this recipe is very dear to my heart. Don't forget to pair it with a beautiful bottle of *vin blanc* . . . or five. If you're trying to #adult, just finish the bottle you cooked with.

1. **Fondue Cheese:** In a large saucepan, heat olive oil over medium-high heat. Add onion and garlic; cover and sweat for about 3 minutes, until translucent. Uncover and add bouillon, water, potato, rice and cashews; bring to a boil. Immediately reduce heat to low, cover and simmer, stirring occasionally, for about 25 to 30 minutes, until rice and potatoes are soft.

2. Remove from heat and transfer contents to a blender. (If you have a small blender and it doesn't all fit, you'll have do this in batches.) Remove the plug in the lid to release steam and blend on High until very smooth. (If you do not have a high-powered blender, this will take longer. Give the motor a break every minute or so, and blend until smooth.) Add sauerkraut brine, nutritional yeast, white wine vinegar, tapioca starch, miso paste, sea salt and mustard powder; blend until smooth.

3. Pour cheese mixture into the pot of a fondue set and heat for 3 to 5 minutes. Whisk in white wine and Kirsch, stirring constantly, for about 3 minutes, until smooth.

4. Serve with warm baguette, roasted potatoes or vegetables, green apples and gherkins or pickled onions.

～ *HACK IT!* ～

Use this cheese in any recipe that calls for melted cheese. Try it in our Très Flawless French Onion soup (page 94), Mason-Dixon Crab Melt (page 149) or jalapeño poppers (page 124).

To get your hands on sauerkraut brine, simply buy a large jar of sauerkraut and drain brine from the fermented cabbage.

**BLENDER
FONDUE SET**

FONDUE CHEESE
1/4 cup olive oil 60 mL
1/4 small onion, chopped 1/4
3 cloves garlic, minced 3
3 vegetable bouillon cubes 3
6 cups water 1.5 L
1 yellow-flesh potato, peeled and cubed 1
1 cup short-grain white rice (Arborio is best) 250 mL
1 cup raw cashews 250 mL
1/2 cup white sauerkraut brine 125 mL
1/2 cup nutritional yeast 125 mL
2 tbsp wine vinegar 30 mL
6 tbsp tapioca starch 90 mL
2 tbsp brown miso paste 30 mL
2 tsp sea salt 10 mL
1 tsp dry mustard powder 5 mL
1/2 cup dry Riesling white wine 125 mL
3 tbsp Kirsch 45 mL

ACCOUTREMENTS
Baguette slices
Roasted potatoes or vegetables
Green apple slices
Gherkins or pickled onions

Better Than Ever Veggie Dogs

SERVES 4

If there is one thing the world hasn't mastered, it's the premade veggie wiener. If, like me, you're tired of those rubbery, pencil-eraser veggie dogs, then FOR THE LOVE OF GOD, make these. I know it sounds crazy, but these perfectly marinated and grilled carrots are the best veggie dogs you'll ever have!

1. In a large resealable bag or plastic container, combine rice vinegar, apple cider vinegar, water, sesame oil, soy sauce, garlic powder, onion powder, ginger, cayenne pepper and black pepper. Set aside.

2. Bring a large pot of water to a boil over high heat. Add carrots and boil for 6 to 8 minutes or until fork-tender. DO NOT OVERCOOK. They should not be mushy, and you want them to hold their shape well.

3. Drain carrots and immediately plunge into a large bowl of ice water. This will stop them from continuing to cook. Let cool for 2 minutes.

4. Using tongs, add carrots to marinade and gently shake to coat. Place bag or plastic container in the fridge for at least 24 hours, but 48 hours is best.

5. Cook veggie dogs on a barbecue (yay, summer!) or a grill pan. If using a barbecue, preheat the barbecue to High. Grill carrots for about 5 minutes, rotating to ensure even cooking, until heated through and slightly charred. If using a grill pan, grease with olive oil and heat over medium-high heat. Add carrots and cook for about 5 minutes, rotating to ensure even cooking, until heated through. For both methods, spoon some marinade over carrots while cooking to create a yummy crusty exterior.

6. Remove from heat and serve on a hot dog bun with your choice of ketchup, mustard, mayo, kimchi, pickled jalapeños, onions and sauerkraut.

BARBECUE OR GRILL PAN

2 tbsp seasoned rice vinegar 30 mL

2 tbsp apple cider vinegar 30 mL

1/4 cup water 60 mL

1 tbsp toasted sesame oil 15 mL

1/4 cup soy sauce or tamari 60 mL

1/2 tsp garlic powder 2 mL

1/2 tsp onion powder 2 mL

1/4 tsp ground ginger 1 mL

1/4 tsp cayenne pepper 1 mL

1/4 tsp freshly ground black pepper 1 mL

4 carrots (roughly the length and thickness of a hot dog), unpeeled and trimmed 4

4 hot dog buns 4

Ketchup

Mustard

Hell No! Egg-Free Mayo (page 50)

Fish-Free Kimchi (page 228)

Pickled jalapeño peppers

Onions

Sauerkraut

Jammin' Jamaican Patties

SERVES 4

I once caught James eating a spicy meat patty in the middle of his 30-day vegan challenge. WTF, those aren't vegan! Jamaican me crazy! Now we have a freezer full of these flaky pastries stuffed with hearty Caribbean filling, ready for reheating when the cravings creep in.

1. **Crust:** In a large bowl, using a fine-mesh sieve, sift together flour, turmeric and salt.

2. Using two knives or a pastry blender, cut in shortening and butter until the mixture becomes crumbly. Working quickly, add small amounts of cold water (2 tbsp/30 mL at a time) to form a firm dough. Do not overwater or overwork. Form dough into a disc, wrap in plastic and refrigerate for at least 1-1/2 hours or overnight.

3. **Filling:** In a large skillet, heat vegan butter over medium-high heat. Add onion and sauté for about 4 minutes, until soft and translucent. Add garlic and ginger and sauté for about 1 minute, until fragrant. Add veggie ground round, turmeric, cumin, allspice, cardamom, thyme and Scotch bonnet, if desired; cook, stirring often, for about 10 minutes, until heated through and spices are fragrant. Add green onions, parsley, vegan Worcestershire, tomatoes and broth; simmer over medium-low heat, stirring occasionally, for about 30 minutes, until most of the liquid has evaporated.

4. Mix in sea salt and pepper. Remove mixture from heat and stir in rum. Taste and season with additional sea salt and pepper. Set aside and let cool.

5. Preheat oven to 400°F (200°C).

6. On a lightly floured surface, roll out pastry dough and cut into circles using round cutter or a cereal bowl (you want the circles to be 6 to 7 inches/15 to 18 cm in diameter).

7. Lightly brush outside edges of each circle with almond milk. Spoon 3 to 4 tbsp (45 to 60 mL) filling onto one half of the circle. Fold other half of pastry over so the edges meet. Pinch to seal, and use the tines of a fork to create a decorative pattern along the edges.

8. Lightly brush top of each patty with almond milk. Place on prepared baking sheet and bake in preheated oven for 30 minutes, until golden brown. Serve with hot sauce on the side for dipping.

FINE-MESH SIEVE
6-INCH (15 CM) ROUND
   CUTTER (OPTIONAL)
BAKING SHEET LINED WITH
   PARCHMENT PAPER
PASTRY CLOTH (OPTIONAL)

CRUST (page 182)
FILLING
2 tbsp vegan butter 30 mL
1 large onion, finely chopped 1
6 garlic cloves, minced 6
1 tbsp minced fresh ginger 15 mL
1 lb veggie ground round or texturized vegetable protein 500 g
1/4 tsp ground turmeric 1 mL
1-1/2 tsp ground cumin 7 mL
3/4 tsp ground allspice 3 mL
1/2 tsp ground cardamom 2 mL
1 tsp dried thyme 5 mL
1 Scotch bonnet pepper, seeded and finely chopped (optional) 1
3 green onions, white and light green parts, finely chopped 3
1 tbsp finely chopped fresh curly parsley 15 mL
2 tbsp vegan Worcestershire 30 mL
3 plum (Roma) tomatoes, peeled and finely chopped 3
3/4 cup All You Need Is Broth (page 34) 175 mL
1-1/2 tsp sea salt 7 mL
1/2 tsp freshly ground black pepper 2 mL
3 tbsp Jamaican rum 45 mL
Sea salt and freshly ground black pepper
Unbleached all-purpose flour
Unsweetened almond milk
Hot sauce to dip (optional)

CRUST

4 cups unbleached all-purpose flour 1 L
1-1/2 tbsp ground turmeric 22 mL
1 tbsp salt 15 mL
1/2 cup cold vegetable shortening, cut into
   cubes 125 mL
1/2 cup cold vegan butter 125 mL
1/2 cup + 2 tbsp ice cold water (approx.) 155 mL

~~~ *HACK IT!* ~~~

You can store any uneaten patties
in the fridge for up to 3 days.

To freeze: Prepare patties through
Step 7. Wrap each patty tightly
in plastic wrap and place in a
freezer bag or container. Freeze for
up to 3 months. Bake patties
as directed in Step 8.

Tofu to Talk a Bao

SERVES 6

As David Chang once said, "Steamed bread + tasty tofu = good eating." Okay, he didn't say tofu; he said meat, but I firmly believe the equation stands strong. The perfect balance of fresh and pickled veg, herbs with gooey sauce and the complementary textures of the crispy tofu with a pillowy bun is absolutely dreamy. Add a side of kimchi fries and you've got, in my opinion, the perfect meal.

1. **Steamed Buns:** Place sugar in a blender and pulse until a superfine but not powdery consistency forms.

2. In a large bowl, whisk together flour and sea salt.

3. In a small bowl, combine yeast, 1 tbsp (15 mL) warm water, and sugar. Let stand until foamy, about 5 minutes.

4. Add yeast mixture, soy milk, rice vinegar, 1 tbsp (15 mL) coconut oil and the remaining 3/4 cup + 2 tbsp (205 mL) water to flour mixture; mix with a wooden spoon until ingredients begin to stick and mix together. Using your hands, knead into a dough. It should be a firm consistency and not sticky. You want as little moisture in this dough as possible.

5. On a lightly floured surface or pastry cloth, knead dough for 10 to 15 minutes, or until smooth.

6. Lightly oil a large glass or metal bowl, add dough and cover with a damp cloth. Let rise for 2 hours.

7. Cut 18 6-inch (15 cm) squares of parchment paper, large enough to hold one bao each.

8. **Pickled Carrot:** In a small bowl, whisk together apple cider vinegar, sugar and sea salt, until smooth. Add carrots and toss to coat. Cover and refrigerate until assembling baos.

9. **Chile Sauce:** In another small bowl, whisk together hoisin sauce, chile oil, rice vinegar and sea salt, until smooth. Cover and refrigerate until assembling baos.

10. **Steamed Buns:** Place dough on a clean counter or pastry cloth and punch it down to flatten. Sprinkle dough with baking powder and knead for 5 minutes, until well incorporated and smooth.

BLENDER OR MINI FOOD PROCESSOR
PASTRY CLOTH (OPTIONAL)
ROLLING PIN
1 CHOPSTICK (OPTIONAL)
1 TO 2 BAKING SHEETS LINED WITH PARCHMENT PAPER
STEAM BASKET
DEEP FRYER OR HEAVY-BOTTOMED SAUCE-PAN FITTED WITH A DEEP-FRY THERMOMETER

STEAMED BUNS
1-1/2 tbsp organic sugar 22 mL
4 cups unbleached all-purpose white flour 1 L
1/2 tsp sea salt 2 mL
1 tsp quick-rising (instant) yeast 5 mL
3/4 cup + 3 tbsp warm water, divided 220 mL
3-1/2 tbsp unsweetened soy milk 52 mL
1 tbsp seasoned rice vinegar 15 mL
1 tbsp softened coconut oil 15 mL
Unbleached all-purpose flour for dusting
1 tsp baking powder 5 mL
Additional softened coconut oil

PICKLED CARROT
1 tbsp apple cider vinegar 15 mL
2 tsp organic sugar 10 mL
1/4 tsp sea salt 1 mL
1 cup julienned carrots 250 mL

11. Using a large knife, cut dough in half and roll each piece with your hands into a long sausage about 1-1/4 inches (3 cm) thick. Cut each sausage into 9 pieces about 1-1/4 inches (3 cm) wide. Using your hands, roll each piece into a ball and let rest, covered with a tea towel, for 2 to 3 minutes.

12. Using a rolling pin, roll out each ball into a 6- by 3-inch (15 by 7.5 cm) oval. Lightly rub coconut oil over each oval. Working one by one, place a chopstick or the end of a small wooden spoon in the center of the oval and fold dough over the chopstick; slowly pull out the chopstick. The two layers should be separated by a pocket of air. Place on baking sheet lined with parchment paper and repeat with the remaining ovals.

13. Cover buns with a tea towel. Move to a warm area of your kitchen and let rise for 1-1/2 hours. They should double in size.

14. Fill a pot with 4 inches (10 cm) of water and bring to a boil. Make sure the steam basket fits inside or on top of the pot: the buns need to sit above the waterline.

15. Place each of 2 to 4 buns (depending on the size of your basket) on a small parchment square and place inside steam basket. Reduce heat to medium-low to maintain a rolling simmer. Steam buns for 8 to 10 minutes, until they puff up. Repeat until all the buns are steamed. Keep an eye on the water level and add more as needed. Place steamed buns on a wire rack until cool to the touch.

16. **Fried Tofu:** In a deep fryer or heavy-bottomed saucepan, heat vegetable oil to 375°F (190°C). If you are frying on the stove, you'll need at least 3 inches (7.5 cm) of oil.

17. Place flour, eggless dip and panko in three separate small bowls. Working in batches, coat tofu in flour, then eggless dip, then panko, shaking off excess. Transfer to a plate until ready to fry.

18. In batches, fry tofu in hot oil for 2 minutes, until crisp and golden brown, turning once. Using a slotted spoon, remove from oil and transfer to a plate lined with paper towel. Let oil heat to 375°F (190°C) between batches.

19. To serve, carefully open each bun and spread with a bit of chile sauce. Add 3 slices of cucumber, 1 to 2 tofu pieces and a bit of pickled carrot. Top with a couple of banana peppers and additional chile sauce and garnish with green onions.

CHILE SAUCE
1/2 cup hoisin sauce 125 mL
2 tbsp Asian chile oil 30 mL
1 tbsp seasoned rice vinegar 15 mL
1/2 tsp sea salt 2 mL

FRIED TOFU
Vegetable oil for frying
1/2 cup unbleached all-purpose flour 125 mL
1 recipe Eggcellent Eggless Dip (page 35) 1
2 cups panko bread crumbs 500 mL
2 packages (7 oz/210 g) smoked tofu, cut into 18 1/2-inch (1 cm) slices 2

GARNISH
1 cucumber, thinly sliced 1
Pickled banana peppers
10 green onions, white and light green parts, sliced 10

HACK IT!

The steamed bun dough can easily be kneaded in a stand mixer with a dough hook, instead of by hand. If you're lazy, like me, I highly recommend it!

Don't want to go through the hassle of making home-made steamed buns? No problem! Just use soft rolls and omit the dough and steaming steps to turn these baos into banh mi sandwiches.

Steaks with Béarnaise Sauce

SERVES 4

As a wee little thing, I would sit on the floor and watch black-and-white videos of Julia Child cooking. I swear, that woman is 100% to blame for my over-the-top kitchen behavior and love of rich food. She also taught me a very important lesson that I may have taken a little too seriously: the only time to eat diet food is while you're waiting for the steak to cook.

1. **Marinade:** In a small bowl, whisk together balsamic vinegar, red wine, olive oil, tamari, vegan Worcestershire and garlic, until well combined.

2. **Steaks:** In a shallow bowl or a large resealable bag, pour marinade over mushroom caps. Marinate for 2 hours or overnight, flipping mushrooms halfway.

3. Meanwhile, prepare steak rub. In a small bowl or jar, combine paprika, oregano, coriander, mustard powder, cumin, sea salt and pepper. Stir or shake to combine. Set aside.

4. Remove mushrooms from marinade, reserving marinade. Pat steak rub all over marinated mushrooms. Cook right away or pop them in the fridge for up to 2 hours if you want to prep dinner ahead of time (#WIN).

5. Preheat oven to 450°F (230°C).

6. Place mushroom caps, gill side up, on a prepared baking sheet. Roast for about 25 minutes, until tender.

7. Heat a cast-iron skillet over medium-high heat. Brush mushroom caps with olive oil. Add 3 to 4 mushrooms, gill side up, to pan and spoon 1 tsp (5 mL) reserved marinade over each mushroom. Cook for 2 to 3 minutes on the first side, flip and cook for 2 to 3 minutes on the second side. Repeat this process 2 to 3 times, until there is minimal to no liquid left in the pan. Remove from heat and slice into 1/2-inch (1 cm) slices. Transfer to a bowl and cover with a plate to keep warm. Repeat with the remaining mushrooms.

8. Arrange one-quarter of the sliced portobellos in a line in the center of each plate and drizzle with béarnaise sauce. Garnish with tarragon, if desired.

BAKING SHEET LINED WITH PARCHMENT PAPER
CAST-IRON OR NONSTICK SKILLET

MARINADE
1/2 cup balsamic vinegar 125 mL
1/2 cup red wine 125 mL
1/4 cup olive oil 60 mL
1/4 cup tamari 60 mL
2 tbsp vegan Worcestershire 30 mL
2 garlic cloves, minced 2

STEAKS
12 large portobello mushrooms, stems removed 12
1/2 tsp paprika 2 mL
1/2 tsp dried oregano 2 mL
1/2 tsp ground coriander 2 mL
1/2 tsp dry mustard powder 2 mL
1/4 tsp ground cumin 1 mL
1/4 tsp sea salt 1 mL
1/4 tsp freshly ground black pepper 1 mL
Olive oil for brushing
1 recipe Weekend at Béarnaise sauce (page 55), warmed 1
Chopped fresh taragon (optional)

HACK IT!

Try to find the largest mushrooms you can. They tend to shrink while cooking so the bigger, the better.

Use these mushroom steaks to replace any dish that requires steak, such as a steak sandwich or fajitas.

I like to serve this with a side of french fries (page 224) or Edgy Veg–approved Brussels sprouts (page 219) — or both!

Street Food-Style Thai Basil Beef

SERVES 4

Pad gra prao is one of Thailand's most beloved street foods. I would know because James lived in Bangkok for a year, where he acquired a habitual need for the stuff. This dish is so good because of the Thai basil, which gives it a peppery kick (and a kick is what James needs to get me a plane ticket to Thailand). It's a household favorite that always delivers — just like my insistence to go to Thailand ASAP.

1. **Rice:** In a large saucepan, combine rice and water. Bring to a boil over high heat. Immediately reduce heat to low, cover with a tight-fitting lid and simmer for 15 minutes, until all the liquid has been absorbed. Remove from heat and let stand, covered, while you prepare the recipe. Use a fork to fluff up the rice when ready to serve.

2. **Basil Beef:** In a food processor, combine garlic, red pepper, red Thai chiles and shallots; pulse until a coarse paste forms.

3. In a large skillet, heat coconut oil over medium-high heat. Add paste and cook, stirring, for about 3 minutes, until fragrant.

4. In a small bowl, whisk together water, 1/4 cup (60 mL) tamari, coconut sugar, 2 tbsp (30 mL) mirin and vegan Worcestershire. Set aside.

5. Add veggie ground round to skillet and cook, breaking, up with a wooden spoon. Add tamari mixture and cook, stirring occasionally, for about 20 minutes, until veggie ground round is steaming and heated through. Make sure to check the amount of liquid in the skillet: if it gets too dry, add a little bit of water. You do not want this to be dry. Add more tamari or mirin to taste.

6. **Serving Sauce:** In a small bowl, whisk together garlic, red Thai chiles, mirin, tamari, lime juice and basil leaves.

7. Once the veggie ground round is heated through, add 1 cup (250 mL) basil leaves. Cover to wilt the basil quickly, about 2 minutes, max.

8. Serve over rice with a side of cucumber slices and a tiny bowl of serving sauce.

FOOD PROCESSOR

RICE
1 cup jasmine rice, rinsed 250 mL
1-1/2 cups water 375 mL

BASIL BEEF
7 garlic cloves, peeled 7
1 red bell pepper, chopped 1
2 red Thai chiles, halved and seeded 2
3 large shallots, roughly chopped 3
3 tbsp coconut oil 45 mL
3 tbsp water 45 mL
1/4 cup tamari (approx.) 60 mL
1 tsp coconut sugar 5 mL
2 tbsp mirin (approx.) 30 mL
3 tbsp vegan Worcestershire 45 mL
2 lbs veggie ground round 1 kg
Sea salt
1 cup packed fresh Thai basil leaves 250 mL

SERVING SAUCE
3 garlic cloves, minced 3
3 red Thai chiles, sliced 3
2 tbsp mirin 30 mL
1/3 cup tamari 75 mL
6 tbsp freshly squeezed lime juice 90 mL
5 fresh Thai basil leaves, roughly chopped 5

1/4 cup sliced cucumber 60 mL

"This Is Takeout" Butter Chicken

SERVES 6

I made this recipe for a YouTube Spaces opening where Lilly Singh was a guest. If you follow her, you know that she's a vegetarian, so she was pretty pumped about our veggie option. She took one bite, looked at James and said, "Wow! This doesn't taste like white people made it!" Don't take my word for it, trust IISuperwomanII's review — this is some Indian takeout–worthy butter chicken.

1. Using a fine-mesh sieve, rinse rice under cold water until water runs clear. Transfer rice to a large bowl of cold water and soak for 30 minutes. Drain.

2. In a large saucepan, heat 2 tbsp (30 mL) peanut oil over medium-high heat. Add onion and sauté for about 3 to 5 minutes, until soft and translucent. Add vegan butter, clove, lemon juice, ginger, garlic, chili powder, 2 tsp (10 mL) garam masala, bay leaves, turmeric, cardamom and cumin; sauté for 1 minute, until fragrant. Add tomato purée and coconut sugar; cook, stirring constantly, for 2 minutes, until it starts to stick to the pot. Reduce heat to low and add non-dairy cream and yogurt; stir until combined. Simmer for 10 minutes, stirring frequently, until heated through. Discard clove and bay leaves. Add salt and black pepper and keep warm over low heat.

3. Transfer rice to a medium saucepan with a tight-fitting lid. Add a pinch of salt and boiling water. Bring to a simmer over medium-high heat and cover. Immediately reduce heat to the lowest setting and cook rice, undisturbed, for 15 minutes. Remove from heat and let stand, covered, while you prepare the rest of the recipe.

4. In a medium skillet, heat remaining 2 tbsp (30 mL) peanut oil over medium heat. Add seitan and cook, stirring often, for about 10 minutes, until heated through.

5. Reduce heat to medium-low. Add cayenne pepper, if using, and remaining 1 tsp (5 mL) garam masala. Add 3 spoonfuls of sauce, tossing to coat seitan. Simmer for about 2 minutes, until liquid has reduced. Add seitan mixture to remaining sauce and stir to coat.

6. Fluff rice with a fork and transfer to a serving dish. Add butter chicken, garnish with cilantro and serve with a slice of naan bread, which works great as spoon, BTW.

FINE-MESH SIEVE

2 cups basmati rice 500 mL
4 tbsp peanut oil, divided 60 mL
1 white onion, finely chopped 1
1/2 cup vegan butter 125 mL
1 whole clove 1
1 tbsp + 1/2 tsp freshly squeezed lemon juice 17 mL
1 tsp ground ginger 5 mL
6 garlic cloves, crushed 6
1 tsp chili powder 5 mL
3 tsp garam masala, divided 15 mL
2 bay leaves 2
1 tbsp ground turmeric 15 mL
1/8 tsp ground cardamom 0.5 mL
2 tsp ground cumin 10 mL
3 cups tomato purée 750 mL
1-1/2 tsp coconut sugar 7 mL
2 cups Essential Non-Dairy Cream (page 49) 500 mL
1/2 cup plain vegan yogurt 125 mL
1/4 tsp salt 1 mL
1/4 tsp freshly ground black pepper 1 mL
3 cups boiling water 750 mL
Become a Master of Seitan: Chicken (Breasts, page 39) cut into bite-size pieces 750 mL
1/8 tsp cayenne pepper (optional) 0.5 mL
1/4 cup fresh cilantro, torn or finely chopped 60 mL
Naan bread

~ *HACK IT!* ~

Don't have premade seitan and don't have the time to make some? No problem! Use a store-bought vegan chicken substitute or fried tofu cubes.

El Cubano Mixto

SERVES 2

Have you ever seen a mouth-watering dish in a movie and are so overcome with drool and hunger that you think: "I *need* that right now"? That happened to me one night while watching Jon Favreau in *Chef*. This fresh roll, piled high with "meat," gooey cheese and a helping of pickles, smothered in mustard and grilled to perfection with plenty of butter, just *had* to be mine.

1. Spread the inside of each half of the roll with Dijon mustard.

2. Layer the cheese, deli slices and pickle medallions on the bottom half of each roll. Top with the other half of each roll and butter outside top of sandwich.

3. If using a panini press, toast the sandwich in the press for about 5 to 7 minutes, until golden brown and cheese is melted. If using a cast-iron skillet, press sandwich down with something heavy, like another cast-iron pan or your old university textbooks (wipe them first, of course), and cook for 5 to 7 minutes on each side or until golden brown and cheese is melted. Serve with a pickle on the side.

PREHEAT PANINI PRESS OR CAST-IRON SKILLET OVER MEDIUM HEAT

2 large hoagie-style rolls, cut in half 2
Dijon mustard
6 vegan cheese slices (I like provolone) 6
10 vegan deli slices (I like Tofurky) 10
8 dill pickle medallions 8
Vegan butter
2 dill pickles 2

HACK IT!

I like to serve these with french fries (page 224) or potato chips.

Le Dip Français

SERVES 2

As James constantly likes to remind me (snob), there is nothing French about this recipe. It's actually an American sandwich that got its name from the bread it's served on. But if any dish near a baguette can be considered French, then hand me a cigarette and a beret and call me a certified *fille française. Salut!*

1. In a large skillet, heat coconut oil over medium heat. Add onion and garlic; sauté for 3 to 5 minutes, until translucent. Reduce heat to medium-low and cook for 30 minutes, stirring every 10 minutes, until onion has caramelized and browned. Set aside.

2. In a small bowl, whisk together mayo, horseradish and pepper. Set aside.

3. In a medium saucepan, heat gravy over medium heat. Add seitan and simmer on low for 10 minutes, stirring occasionally, until seitan is heated through. Remove from heat.

4. Arrange 4 baguette pieces, cut side up, on a baking sheet. Toast in preheated oven for about 5 minutes, until golden brown.

5. Remove bread from oven. Turn oven to Broil. Spread the 2 top halves of the baguette with horseradish mayo and the 2 bottom halves with Dijon mustard. Using a slotted spoon, pile seitan slices on bottom half of each baguette, followed by 2 slices of vegan cheese. Place the 2 bottom halves in the oven and broil for about 1 minute, until cheese begins to bubble and is melty.

6. Transfer leftover gravy to small ramekins or bowls.

7. Remove sandwiches from the oven and top with caramelized onions and top halves. Serve with warm gravy on the side.

PREHEAT OVEN TO 450°F (230°C)

1 tbsp coconut oil 15 mL
1 sweet onion, sliced 1
1 garlic clove, minced 1
3 tbsp Hell No! Egg-Free Mayo (page 50) 45 mL
1 tbsp prepared horseradish 15 mL
1/4 tsp freshly ground black pepper 1 mL
1 recipe Liquid Gold Gravy (page 56), cornstarch omitted 1
2 cups sliced Seitan Mastery 2.0: Beef (page 40) 500 mL
2/3 French baguette, cut in half and down the center 2/3
2 tbsp Dijon mustard 30 mL
4 vegan cheese slices (I like provolone) 4

~~~ HACK IT! ~~~

Don't have any seitan beef on hand? Just make this recipe with the same amount of sliced portobello mushrooms. In a large skillet, heat 2 tbsp (30 mL) olive oil over medium heat. Sauté mushrooms for about 5 minutes on each side, until lightly browned. Proceed with Step 3.

Use leftover baguette in Shakshuka, Habibi! (page 78), French Bistro Salad (page 109) or Easy Cheesy Fondue (page 178)!

Shredded Hogtown Jackfruit

SERVES 4

Sure, this sandwich isn't the prettiest girl at the prom, but if this soft bakery bun piled sky-high with BBQ sauce, tossed-jackfruit-as-pulled-pork and tangy coleslaw doesn't leave you smiling like a Texan in a gun range, then we just can't be friends. Plus it's 90% veg — so you can go for seconds while also working on that bikini body. Or, better yet, put it in your body while wearing a bikini.

1. In a large bowl, combine 1 tbsp (15 mL) coconut oil, paprika, chili powder and maple syrup. Add jackfruit and stir gently to coat. Cover and marinate for a minimum of 2 hours or up to 24 hours in the fridge.

2. In a large skillet, heat remaining 1 tbsp (15 mL) coconut oil over medium heat. Add onion and garlic; sauté for about 3 to 5 minutes, until translucent. Add water and jackfruit with any remaining marinade; simmer for 10 minutes, stirring frequently, until liquid has reduced slightly. Cover and reduce heat to medium low. Simmer for an additional 10 minutes, stirring occasionally, until tender.

3. Reduce heat to low. Using a potato masher or fork, break up jackfruit. Cover and cook for an additional 15 minutes, stirring frequently, until all the liquid has evaporated. Remove from heat.

4. Add BBQ sauce and toss to coat jackfruit. Add more BBQ sauce if you like your pulled pork really messy and gooey.

5. Spoon jackfruit onto bottom halves of buns. Top with slaw and close buns. Serve.

2 tbsp melted coconut oil, divided 30 mL
2 tsp paprika 10 mL
2 tsp chili powder 10 mL
1 tbsp pure maple syrup 15 mL
2 cans (each 20 oz/590 g) young jackfruit in water, drained and rinsed 2
1 small onion, finely sliced 1
3 cloves garlic, minced 3
1/2 cup water 125 mL
3/4 cup vegan-friendly BBQ sauce (approx.) 175 mL
4 hamburger buns 4
3 cups Eat the Rainbow . . . Slaw (page 113) 750 mL

～～ *HACK IT!* ～～～～～～

Serve this BBQ jackfruit in corn tortillas topped with pickled jalapeños for quick and easy carnitas.

Go wild and add mac and cheese (page 170) on top of the jackfruit for the ultimate frankensandwich.

Try this with prepared Korean BBQ sauce, and you've got Korean barbecue at home.

No Fuss BLT

SERVES 1

The BLT, while seemingly simple, has a complex flavor profile that is easily ruined by choosing the wrong ingredients. The bread should either be super high-quality bakery or soft white sliced bread — no in-between stuff, I mean it. Also, we aren't savages, so it must be toasted. Don't try getting fancy with condiments. It's mayo or nothin'.

1. Spread mayo on one side of each piece of toasted bread. Top bottom slice with lettuce and tomatoes and season with sea salt and pepper. Sprinkle with bacon, top with second slice of toast and cut in half to serve.

HACK IT!

Try this with a couple of slices of avocado for sheer and utter perfection.

1 tbsp Hell No! Egg-Free Mayo (page 50) 15 mL
2 bread slices of choice, toasted 2
2 iceberg lettuce leaves 2
1/2 heirloom tomato, sliced 1/2
Sea salt and freshly ground pepper
2 tbsp Coconut Bacon (page 46) 30 mL

The Pho-ritto

SERVES 4

All the deliciousness of a bowl of pho, but in a convenient handheld burrito. This recipe is for all those times you tried eating pho in a crowded subway.

1. Pour pho broth into a small saucepan and bring to a boil over high heat. Immediately reduce heat to low, cover and simmer until ready to use.

2. In a medium skillet, heat peanut oil over medium heat. Add onion and garlic; sauté for about 3 to 5 minutes, until translucent. Add jalapeños; sauté for about 5 minutes, until bright green. Add bean sprouts and 2 tbsp (30 mL) pho broth, stirring to coat completely. Sauté for about 1 minute, until spouts are slightly soft but still have a slight crunch to them. Remove from heat.

3. Bring a large pot of salted water to a boil. Add rice noodles and cook for about 3 to 5 minutes, stirring constantly for the first 2 minutes, until tender. Drain and set aside.

4. Bring simmering pho broth back up to a boil over high heat. Add seitan and cook for about 30 seconds, until heated through. Using a slotted spoon, remove seitan and place on a plate without paper towel.

5. In a small bowl, whisk together cornstarch and water.

6. Whisk cornstarch into remaining broth. Reduce heat to low and let broth simmer for 3 to 5 minutes to thicken slightly.

7. Soften tortillas slightly by microwaving them for 10 to 15 seconds, or warm them one by one in a large, dry skillet for 25 seconds, flipping once.

8. Divide seitan between tortillas. Drizzle each with 1 tbsp (15 mL) Sriracha sauce and 1 tbsp (15 mL) hoisin sauce. Evenly divide sautéed vegetables, basil, cilantro, green onion and rice noodles between tortillas. Spoon 1 tbsp (15 mL) pho broth overtop each. Fold edge of each tortilla up and over filling, toward the center. Roll bottom of tortilla toward top, like a burrito.

9. Heat a large, dry skillet over medium heat. Arrange burritos, seam side down, in batches as necessary, and toast for 1 to 2 minutes, turning once, until golden brown.

10. Serve each pho-ritto with a small ramekin or bowl of pho broth as a dip, along with extra Sriracha sauce and hoisin sauce.

3 cups pho broth (page 85) 750 mL

1 tbsp peanut oil 15 mL

1 white onion, sliced 1

1 large garlic clove, minced 1

2 jalapeño peppers, sliced lengthwise 2

1 cup bean sprouts 250 mL

6 oz vermicelli rice noodles 175 g

2 cups thinly sliced Seitan Mastery 2.0: Beef (page 40) 500 mL

1 tbsp cornstarch 15 mL

2 tbsp water 30 mL

4 large flour tortillas 4

1/4 cup Sriracha sauce 60 mL

1/4 cup hoisin sauce 60 mL

1/2 cup Thai basil, chopped 125 mL

1/2 cup fresh cilantro, chopped 125 mL

1 green onion, white and light green parts, sliced 1

Sriracha sauce

Hoisin sauce

Crunchy Taco Wrap Supreme

SERVES 4

One person in my relationship spent their high-school lunch money almost exclusively at Taco Bell. Hint — it wasn't me. I, on the other hand, somehow made it to my mid-twenties never having consumed the stuff. Then our YouTube audience requested this culinary masterpiece: a tortilla filled with spiced taco meat, nacho cheese and a crisp tostada. YAAASS QUEEEEN (that was from James).

1. In a large skillet, heat olive oil over medium-high heat. Add veggie ground round, water and taco seasoning; cook for about 10 minutes, stirring occasionally, until liquid has evaporated. Set aside.

2. Microwave tortillas for 10 seconds, or warm them one by one in a large, dry skillet for 25 seconds, flipping once.

3. One at a time, lay out tortillas and spread with a couple of dollops of sour cream in the center. Top each with 1/4 to 1/2 cup (60 to 125 mL) veggie ground round, depending on size of your tortilla. Place tostada shell on top of veggie ground round and spread 2 tbsp (30 mL) cheese sauce on top. Evenly distribute diced tomatoes and shredded lettuce on top of cheese sauce.

4. Starting at one side, fold a small section of each tortilla up over the ingredients, toward the center. Move your way around entire tortilla, tightly layering edges, until all edges are folded inward. There will be a spot left open in center. This is okay as long as it's not too large (more than 2 fingers wide). If it is, just fill it in with a cut piece of another flour tortilla.

5. Heat a large, dry skillet over medium-low heat. One at a time, gently place wrap, seam side down, on heated pan. Toast for 3 to 5 minutes, until golden brown. Do not flip too early or else the wrap will fall apart. Flip wrap and toast for another 2 to 3 minutes, until golden brown.

6. Serve with a side of hot sauce or salsa to dip, if desired.

1 tbsp olive oil 15 mL
2 cups veggie ground round or minced Seitan Mastery 2.0: Beef (page 40) 500 mL
1/4 cup water 60 mL
1 package (1 oz/30 g) taco seasoning 1
4 large flour tortillas 4
1/2 cup Burrito-Worthy Sour Cream (page 51) 125 mL
4 tostada shells 4
1/2 cup The Art of Cheese Sauce (page 52) 125 mL
2 plum (Roma) tomatoes, diced 2
1/4 head iceberg lettuce, shredded 1/4
Hot sauce (optional)
1 recipe Austin-Tacious Roasted Salsa (page 150; optional) 1

HACK IT!

Can't find tostadas? Use corn tortillas instead. Just heat oven to 400°F (200°C), place on a baking sheet and bake for 5 to 10 minutes, until crispy. Homemade tostadas!

Saint Francesco's Eggplant Sandwich

SERVES 4

So far as we can tell, the Italian veal and eggplant sandwich is a Toronto Italian thing. Sure, Italian sandwiches are popular in many places, but the way we do it here in the "6ix" is a little different. The eggplant is coated in seasoned bread crumbs, deep-fried until golden brown, doused in marinara sauce and then nestled into a soft bun with fried peppers. It's perfect for a raging appetite on a cold fall day. Drake EP sold separately.

1. Place eggplant rounds in a colander and sprinkle with 1/2 tsp (2 mL) salt; toss to coat. Let stand for 20 minutes to draw out the liquid and reduce bitterness. Blot excess moisture with paper towel.

2. In a deep fryer or heavy-bottomed saucepan, heat vegetable oil to 375°F (190°C). If you are frying on the stove, you'll need roughly 2 to 3 inches (5 to 7.5 cm) of oil.

3. In a large skillet, heat 2 tbsp (30 mL) olive oil over medium-high heat. Add mushrooms and 1/4 tsp (1 mL) salt; cook for about 10 minutes, stirring occasionally, until all the liquid has evaporated and mushrooms are tender and browned. Reduce heat to low, to keep warm.

4. In a small skillet, heat remaining 1 tbsp (15 mL) olive oil over medium-high heat. Add jalapeños; sauté for about 5 minutes, stirring occasionally, until jalapeños are soft and bright green. Reduce heat to low, to keep warm.

5. In a medium bowl, whisk together bread crumbs, basil, oregano, parsley and pepper. Set aside.

6. Place eggless dip in a small bowl. Set aside.

7. Working in batches, dip eggplant into eggless dip and coat completely in bread crumbs, shaking off excess. Fry eggplant in oil for about 4 minutes per batch, until lightly golden and cooked through, flipping once. Remove from oil and place on a plate lined with paper towels. Pat off excess oil with paper towel. Let oil heat to 375°F (190°C) between batches.

DEEP FRYER OR HEAVY-BOTTOMED SAUCE-PAN FITTED WITH A DEEP-FRY THERMOMETER

1 **medium** eggplant, peeled and cut into 1/2-inch (1 cm) rounds 1

3/4 **tsp** salt, divided 3 mL

3 **tbsp** olive oil, divided 45 mL

3 **cups** sliced cremini mushrooms 750 mL

4 **jalapeño** peppers, thinly sliced 4

2 **cups** dry Italian-style seasoned bread crumbs 500 mL

1 **tsp** dried basil 5 mL

1 **tsp** dried oregano 5 mL

1 **tsp** dried parsley 5 mL

1/4 **tsp** freshly ground black pepper 1 mL

1 **recipe** Eggcellent Eggless Dip (page 35) 1

Vegetable oil for frying

4 **crusty** kaiser buns, sliced in half 4

1 **cup** Marinara Italiano (page 57), warm 250 mL

8 **slices** vegan mozzarella cheese or 1/2 cup (125 mL) Fondue Cheese (page 178), warmed 8

Spiced olives

8. To assemble sandwiches, place 2 to 3 pieces of eggplant on the bottom half of each bun, followed by 3 to 4 tbsp (45 to 60 mL) marinara sauce, 2 slices of cheese (or a heavy layer of cheese sauce), mushrooms, jalapeños and the top of the bun. If you like it messy, add an extra tbsp (15 mL) marinara sauce. Serve with a side of spiced olives.

HACK IT!

Replace the eggplant with my veal parmigiana (page 173), and you've got yourself a veal sandwich.

Turn down the heat by using red bell peppers instead of jalapeños, but don't forget to flash-fry in Step 4.

The Mack Daddy

SERVES 2

The Big Mac is an unquestionable fast-food icon, woven into the fabric of our society like the mason jar and the Kardashians. We couldn't call ourselves *the* comfort-food vegans if we didn't include our version with the famous two non-beef patties, special sauce, lettuce, cheese, pickles and onions on a sesame bun, now could we?

1. **Mack Daddy Sauce:** In a small bowl, whisk together mayo, French dressing, relish, onion, white vinegar, sugar and sea salt. Cover and refrigerate until ready to use.

2. **Burgers:** Heat a grill pan over medium-high heat. Brush with coconut oil. Cook burgers for 3 to 4 minutes on each side, until heated through (or according to package instructions if different). Remove from heat and place in a medium bowl. Cover with a plate to keep warm.

3. Split each bun in half. Discard the two tops (or keep for another use) and use the bottoms as the middle bun of the Mack Daddy burgers.

4. Place three bun layers, cut side down, on the grill pan. Heat for 1 minute, until golden. Repeat with the remaining buns.

5. Spread 1/2 to 1 tbsp (7 to 15 mL) Mack Daddy sauce over the bottom piece of each bun. Add about 1 tsp (5 mL) minced onion, 2 tbsp (30 mL) lettuce, 1 cheese slice, 1 veggie burger and 3 pickle medallions. Top with the middle portion of the bun and spread with another 1/2 to 1 tbsp (7 to 15 mL) Mack Daddy sauce, 1 tsp (5 mL) minced onion, another 2 tbsp (30 mL) lettuce, 3 pickle medallions, second veggie burger and burger top. Repeat with second burger.

6. Serve with a side of fries (page 224), wait for an hour and then go to a spin class.

~~ HACK IT! ~~

If you have thick burger patties, use only 2 and halve them by cutting through the center to make them thin.

Easily make dirty animal fries by topping fries with Mack Daddy sauce, minced onions and a crumbled veggie patty on top. It's a sloppy and delicious mess.

GRILL PAN

MACK DADDY SAUCE

1/4 cup Hell No! Egg-Free Mayo (page 50) 60 mL

1 tbsp French salad dressing 15 mL

1 tbsp sweet relish 15 mL

1-1/2 tsp minced white onion 7 mL

1/2 tsp white vinegar 2 mL

1/2 tsp organic sugar 2 mL

1/8 tsp sea salt 0.5 mL

BURGERS

1 tbsp coconut oil 15 mL

4 thin veggie burgers 4

4 sesame seed hamburger buns 4

1/2 small onion, minced 1/2

1/2 cup shredded iceberg lettuce 125 mL

2 slices vegan American-style cheese 2

12 dill pickle medallions 12

Cheesy Stuffed Portobello Burgers

SERVES 2

Do you have a moment to talk about my savior, the portobello burger? Sometimes eating a really good burger can feel like a religious experience. This is the burger to redeem all burgers: cheesy goodness sandwiched between two portobello mushrooms that have been breaded and deep-fried and placed on a bun with crisp toppings. Let me convert you.

1. **Burgers:** Line a plate with two layers of paper towel. Place mushroom caps on top, add two more layers of paper towel and weigh down with a second plate. Micro-wave until mushrooms are completely tender, about 4 minutes. Let stand for 10 minutes or until cool enough to handle. Remove excess moisture from mushrooms by pressing them between three layers of paper towel with your hands.

2. Place 2 mushroom caps, gill side up, on two separate squares of plastic wrap large enough to wrap around the mushrooms. Divide the cheese in half, and squish it together in your hands to form 2 cheese balls. Place a cheese ball on top of each mushroom cap and press down. Top each with a second mushroom cap, gill side down. Twist plastic wrap tightly at the top like a lollipop and press with your hands to form burgers. Transfer to the fridge while you prepare the rest of the recipe.

3. **Burger Sauce:** If using, in a small bowl, whisk together mayo, ketchup, pickle juice, mustard, paprika, garlic powder, onion powder and pinch of cayenne. Set aside.

4. In a deep fryer or heavy-bottomed saucepan, heat pea-nut oil to 375°F (190°C). If you are frying on the stove, you'll need at least 3 inches (7.5 cm) of oil.

5. Place eggless dip, flour and bread crumbs into three separate small bowls. Remove portobello burgers from plastic wrap. (If burgers come apart, secure with toothpicks.) Dip portobello burgers into flour, then into eggless dip, then into bread crumbs. Dip in eggless dip again and then into bread crumbs for a second time. Transfer to a plate lined with parchment paper and let rest for 3 to 5 minutes.

DEEP FRYER OR HEAVY-BOTTOMED SAUCE-PAN FITTED WITH A DEEP-FRY THERMOMETER

BURGERS
4 portobello mushroom caps, each 4 inches (10 cm) across, stems and gills removed 4
1/2 cup grated vegan Cheddar 125 mL

BURGER SAUCE (OPTIONAL)
1/4 cup Hell No! Egg-Free Mayo (page 50) 60 mL
1 tbsp ketchup 15 mL
1 tsp dill pickle juice 5 mL
1 tsp mustard 5 mL
1/4 tsp paprika 1 mL
1/4 tsp garlic powder 1 mL
1/4 tsp onion powder 1 mL
Cayenne pepper

Peanut oil for frying
1 recipe Eggcellent Eggless Dip (page 35) 1
1/2 cup unbleached all-purpose flour 125 mL
1 cup panko bread crumbs 250 mL
2 burger buns 2
2 green-leaf lettuce leaves 2
1 plum (Roma) tomato, sliced 1

6. Place mushrooms in hot oil and fry for about 4 to 5 minutes, flipping after 2 minutes, until golden brown on both sides. Remove from hot oil and transfer to a plate lined with paper towel.

7. Place lettuce, tomato and cooked burgers on the bottom half of each bun. Spread burger sauce, if using, on top bun. Close your sandwich and enjoy!

Chick-Fillet Deluxe

SERVES 4

James swears that the legendary Chick-fil-A sandwich is the best chicken sandwich ever created. He challenged me to recreate this "magical work of art" when he first agreed to try out this whole vegan thing. Naturally I agreed, because relationships are totally about compromise to get what you want in the end. After many exhausting attempts with a taste tester who kept telling me it wasn't *quite* right, James finally proclaimed that I had nailed it — you couldn't tell the difference at all. You're welcome!

1. In a shallow bowl, combine 2-1/2 cups (625 mL) pickle juice and 1/2 tsp (2 mL) cayenne pepper. Add burgers, making sure they are submerged in the marinade, and marinate for 1 hour.

2. In a deep fryer or heavy-bottomed saucepan, heat peanut oil to 325°F (160°C). If you are frying on the stove, you will need about 4 to 6 inches (10 to 15 cm) of oil.

3. In a small bowl, whisk together remaining 1/4 cup (60 mL) pickle juice and almond milk. Set aside.

4. In a medium bowl, whisk together flour, confectioners' sugar, remaining 1 tbsp (15 mL) cayenne, paprika, peppercorns, chili powder, sea salt, baking powder and garlic powder. Set aside.

5. Coat each burger in the flour mixture, then toss it into the milk mixture, coating evenly on all sides. Coat generously in flour mixture again.

6. In batches, place burgers in hot oil. Fry for about 5 to 8 minutes, flipping occasionally, or until the outside is crisp and golden brown. Using tongs, remove burgers from oil and place on a plate lined with paper towel.

7. Heat a large, dry skillet over low heat. Toast buns, cut side down, for about 1 to 2 minutes, until golden brown.

8. Remove buns from the pan. Place vegan cheese on bottom half of each bun and top with fried chicken and 4 pickle slices. Serve immediately with your favorite hot sauce, if desired.

HACK IT!

We are often too lazy to make burgers from scratch. If you're hard up for time, you can use a store-bought vegan chicken cutlet or burger substitute or smoked tofu.

PREHEAT OVEN TO 350°F (180°C)

DEEP FRYER OR HEAVY-BOTTOMED SAUCE-PAN FITTED WITH A DEEP-FRY THERMOMETER

2-3/4 cups dill pickle juice, divided 685 mL

1 tbsp + 1/2 tsp cayenne pepper, divided 17 mL

4 Become a Master of Seitan: Chicken (Burgers, page 39) 4

3/4 cup unsweetened almond milk 175 mL

2 cups unbleached all-purpose flour 500 mL

1/3 cup organic confectioners' (icing) sugar 75 mL

1 tbsp + 1/2 tsp paprika, divided 17 mL

2 tsp cracked black peppercorns 10 mL

1 tsp chili powder 5 mL

1 tsp sea salt 5 mL

1 tsp baking powder 5 mL

1 tsp garlic powder 5 mL

Peanut oil for frying

BURGERS

4 white burger buns 4

4 slices vegan cheese (I like provolone) 4

16 dill pickle medallions 16

Hot sauce (optional)

On The Side

/ôn THə sīd/ *phrase*

1. In addition to one's primary employment or as a supplemental source of income • *Candice worked at an ad agency, but she was making money from YouTube on the side.*
2. Secretly, usually regarding a relationship in addition to one's legal spouse or partner • *Matt is dating Jill, but he has a mistress on the side.*
3. Served separately from and in addition to the main dish • *"Can I get the fully loaded burrito (hold the guac) with the guacamole and some chips on the side?"*

NOBODY GIVES SIDES THE PROPER ATTENTION. With the tiniest amount of effort, they can be the tastiest part of your meal and won't get you into trouble with your day job or your partner. For the love of God, just don't ever serve your greens boiled.

Herb-Roasted Wild Mushrooms

SERVES 4 AS A SIDE

I am mad about mushrooms — something I've made incredibly apparent in this book you're holding. Roasting them with herbs to create a mouth-watering, meaty side dish is my idea of simple perfection. Try these on top of a crostini or pizza (page 154), with Gnocchi Puttanesca! (page 165) or mixed into salads. As you can see, I can *and will* find a place for them in every meal. It's no *truffle* at all. I think I might go eat some right now; I have *mush room* in my belly.

1. In a large bowl, stir together garlic, olive oil, thyme, rosemary and marjoram. Add mushrooms, season with 1/4 tsp (1 mL) each sea salt and pepper, and toss until well coated.

2. Spread mushrooms on a prepared baking sheet and set the bowl aside — dishes are the worst, so let's save this one for later! Bake mushrooms in the preheated oven for 20 minutes, toss, and return to the oven for an additional 10 minutes, until dark in color and slightly shriveled.

3. Return mushrooms back to the same large bowl and toss with parsley. Season to taste with sea salt and pepper, if necessary.

PREHEAT OVEN TO 450°F (230°C)
RIMMED BAKING SHEET LINED WITH PARCHMENT PAPER

2 garlic cloves, minced 2
1/4 cup olive oil 60 mL
1 tsp dried thyme 5 mL
1 tsp dried rosemary 5 mL
1/2 tsp dried marjoram 2 mL
1-1/2 lbs mixed mushrooms (my faves are cremini, shiitake and oyster), sliced 750 g
Sea salt and freshly ground black pepper
2 tbsp flat-leaf (Italian) parsley, finely chopped 30 mL

Brussels Sprouts That Don't Suck

SERVES 4

Who on God's green earth decided to collectively traumatize kids by serving them boiled Brussels sprouts (blech!)? Until I met James's mom, Lea, I absolutely despised the things. But this woman — she knew how to cook 'em! As far as I'm concerned, her recipe, which I've replicated here, is the only acceptable way to serve them: crispy, slightly charred and covered in garlicky oil. Otherwise, they're Satan's sprouts.

1. Fill a large stock pot halfway with water and bring to a boil. Add Brussels sprouts and boil for 2 minutes, until bright green in color. Drain and let drip-dry for 10 minutes. (Excess water will prevent these bad boys from crisping, and crisping is key here.)

2. In a large bowl, whisk together olive oil, garlic, 1/2 tsp (2 mL) sea salt and 1/4 tsp (1 mL) pepper.

3. Slice Brussels sprouts in half. Add to the oil mixture and toss to coat.

4. Transfer to a prepared baking sheet in a single layer and bake in the preheated oven for 15 minutes. Flip Brussels sprouts and bake for another 15 minutes, until edges are lightly charred and crisp. Be sure to keep an eye on your sprouts while baking: they can go from done to BURNT in a matter of seconds. Season to taste with sea salt and pepper, if necessary.

PREHEAT OVEN TO 400°F (200°C)
BAKING SHEET LINED WITH PARCHMENT PAPER

1-1/2 lbs Brussels sprouts, trimmed 750 g
1/4 cup olive oil 60 mL
4 garlic cloves, minced 4
Sea salt and freshly ground black pepper

~~ HACK IT! ~~

Serve these with our portobello steaks (page 188) or Gnocchi Puttanesca! (page 165) for a delicious and satisfying meal.

The outer Brussels sprout leaves will be extra dark and crispy after you finish roasting, almost like little chips — this is sprout gold!

Crispy, Salty, Oh So Savory Okra Chips

SERVES 4 AS A SIDE

Our love for Indian food has taken us to some interesting places. One of those places is Dishoom in London, England. *Let me clarify: I sat at home while James went there.* I still remember the night James introduced me to okra fries over a loud, distorted FaceTime. They're like french fries, but with a richer mouth feel and curry flavors. Once we finally "met," I couldn't live another day without them in my life, especially when I'm making our bomb butter chicken (page 192).

1. In a deep fryer or heavy-bottomed saucepan, heat vegetable oil to 375°F (190°C). If you are frying on the stove, you'll need roughly 2 to 3 inches (5 to 7.5 cm) of oil.

2. In a large bowl, whisk together chickpea flour, corn flour, garlic powder, ginger, chili powder, cumin, turmeric and 1/4 tsp (1 mL) sea salt. Set aside.

3. In another large bowl, combine okra and eggless dip; toss to coat. Transfer okra to the flour mixture and toss to coat.

4. In batches, fry okra in the hot oil for 4 to 5 minutes, until light brown and crispy. Using a slotted spoon, remove okra, allowing the excess oil to drip off, and place on a plate lined with paper towel.

5. Sprinkle with garam masala and a pinch of sea salt. Serve and dream of London and Dishoom.

DEEP FRYER OR HEAVY-BOTTOMED SAUCE-PAN FITTED WITH A DEEP-FRY THERMOMETER

Vegetable oil for frying
1/2 cup chickpea flour 125 mL
1/3 cup corn flour 75 mL
1 tsp garlic powder 5 mL
1-1/2 tsp ground ginger 7 mL
1 tsp chili powder 5 mL
1 tsp ground cumin 5 mL
1/4 tsp ground turmeric 1 mL
Sea salt
1 lb okra, trimmed and sliced in half lengthwise 500 g
1 recipe Eggcellent Eggless Dip (page 35) 1
Garam masala

Garlicky Green Beans to Keep the Vampires Away

SERVES 4 AS A SIDE

This is our go-to we-need-greens-in-this-meal side dish. I like 'em crunchy and James likes 'em dead, like baby-food mush. In this debate I always win because, well, I'm the one cooking. I'll agree to making him baby food when we have, you know, a baby. Serve these super-garlicky beans alongside our Spaghetti and Neat Balls, Bro (page 166), Italian Bakery Veal Parmigiana (page 173) or Steaks with Béarnaise Sauce (page 188), and you'll never have to worry about running into a vampire again.

1. Bring a large pot of salted water to a boil.

2. Add beans and boil for 3 minutes, until they turn bright green. Drain.

3. Quickly plunge beans into a bowl filled with ice water for 1 minute, then drain. Let drip-dry for 15 minutes.

4. In a large bowl, stir together olive oil, garlic, sea salt and pepper. Add beans and toss to coat.

5. In a large skillet, sauté beans over medium-high heat for 4 to 6 minutes, stirring constantly, until garlic is crispy and the beans have seared brown spots. Remove from heat and serve.

1-1/2 lbs green beans, trimmed 750 g
2 tbsp olive oil 30 mL
4 garlic cloves, minced 4
1/4 tsp sea salt 1 mL
1/4 tsp freshly ground black pepper 1 mL

Potatoes Served in the French Manner

SERVES 4 TO 6 AS A SIDE

French fries are made from potatoes, and potatoes are vegetables. Therefore, french fries are vegetables. We eat a lot of vegetables . . .

1. Place potatoes in a large bowl and add enough water to cover completely. Soak for at least 1 hour or up to 24 hours in the fridge. (I soak mine overnight.)

2. Drain potatoes and allow them to drip-dry for 15 minutes. Lay them on the first prepared baking sheet. Blot with additional paper towels to dry completely.

3. Meanwhile, in a deep fryer or heavy-bottomed saucepan, heat vegetable oil to 350°F (180°C). If you are frying on the stove, you'll need at least 3 to 4 inches (7.5 to 10 cm) of oil.

4. Add 2 handfuls of potatoes to hot oil, ensuring that they are covered completely. Par-cook potatoes for 5 to 7 minutes, until they are very light brown. Using tongs, remove potatoes, gently shaking off excess oil, and drain on the second prepared baking sheet. Repeat until all the potatoes are par-cooked.

5. Raise oil temperature to 375°F (190°C). Fry potatoes, in batches, for about 2 minutes, until golden brown. Using tongs, remove potatoes, gently shaking off excess oil, and place in a mixing bowl lined with paper towel. Sprinkle with sea salt, paprika and pepper, adding more to taste, if desired.

DEEP FRYER OR
HEAVY-BOTTOMED SAUCE-
PAN FITTED WITH A DEEP-
FRY THERMOMETER
2 BAKING SHEETS LINED
WITH PAPER TOWELS

4 large russet potatoes (roughly 2 lbs/1 kg total), peeled and cut into matchsticks 4
Vegetable oil for frying
1 tbsp sea salt 15 mL
1 tbsp paprika 15 mL
1 tsp freshly ground black pepper 5 mL

HACK IT!

The skinnier you cut the potatoes, the crispier your fries will be.

Do not skip soaking in Step 1. Soaking helps remove the excess starch from the potatoes and keeps them from oxidizing.

Try seasoning your fries with a variety of spices, like Old Bay, Cajun spice or za'atar.

Edgy Roasted Veg

SERVES 4 AS A SIDE

If I'm honest with myself, there's nothing "edgy" about roasted veg. The creamy, herbed tahini sauce drizzled on top makes these veggies pop with excitement instead of being cast aside as an afterthought. This dish got its name from our weekly family potlucks. Every Tuesday (okay, not every, but we try) we host a potluck with our neighbors. We're often reminded, "Don't forget the edgy veggies!"

1. In a large bowl, combine cauliflower, broccoli, Jerusalem artichokes and onion; add olive oil and toss to coat. Season with 1/4 tsp (1 mL) each salt and pepper.

2. Arrange vegetables in a single layer on a prepared baking sheet and roast for 30 to 40 minutes, until lightly browned. The edges should be slightly charred and the vegetables soft when pierced with a fork.

3. Meanwhile, in a blender, combine tahini, garlic, 1/4 cup (60 mL) parsley, lemon juice, 1/2 tsp (2 mL) salt and water; blend on High until smooth. Set aside.

4. In the same large bowl, combine roasted vegetables, lemon zest, paprika and remaining 1 cup (250 mL) parsley; toss to coat. Sprinkle with sea salt and pepper to taste.

5. Transfer to a platter and drizzle with tahini sauce. Reserve some sauce for dipping (yes, I want you to dip your already-sauced veggies!).

~~~ HACK IT! ~~~

Jerusalem artichokes are sold in the produce section of a lot of large supermarkets. If Jerusalem artichokes are out of season or aren't available where you live, substitute potatoes, parsnips or turnips.

In my opinion, the charred bits on roasted veggies are the tastiest. Trust me, you want those! Keep roasting until you see the vegetables start to char around the edges.

PREHEAT OVEN TO 425°F (220°C)
BAKING SHEET LINED WITH PARCHMENT PAPER
BLENDER OR FOOD PROCESSOR

1 head cauliflower, cut into florets 1

1 head broccoli, cut into florets 1

2 cups sliced (1/4 inch/0.5 cm thick) Jerusalem artichokes 500 mL

1 large onion, sliced into half-moons 1

2 tbsp olive oil 30 mL

Sea salt and freshly ground black pepper

1/4 cup tahini 60 mL

1 garlic clove, crushed 1

1-1/4 cups curly parsley, finely chopped, divided 310 mL

1 tsp finely grated lemon zest 5 mL

1 tbsp freshly squeezed lemon juice 15 mL

2 tbsp water 30 mL

1/4 tsp hot paprika 1 mL

Fish-Free Kimchi

MAKES 4 CUPS (1 L)

I take my obsessions very seriously. For example, my obsession with llamas has manifested itself in random ceramic kitchen tools and mugs, and my obsession with kimchi has created an evening mantra for James: "If you're going to insist on eating smelly food, do it outside." Some have ketchup, I have kimchi. Sure, it's smelly, but it's also spicy, rich in flavor and effing delicious. Enjoy as a side, as a sauce or on top of a burger or Better Than Ever Veggie Dogs (page 181) as a condiment.

1. In a large mixing bowl, combine cabbage and sea salt; massage for 8 to 10 minutes, until cabbage begins to soften. Cover with distilled water and place a plate (smaller than the bowl) on top of the cabbage, then weigh it down with a stack of plates or a few cans of beans. Let stand for 2 hours.

2. In a small bowl, whisk together garlic, ginger, hot pepper flakes, vegan Worcestershire, lime juice, sugar, kelp and 3 tbsp (45 mL) distilled water. Set aside.

3. Drain cabbage and rinse very well; let stand in a colander for 15 minutes to drip-dry.

4. Squeeze the remaining water from cabbage. In a large bowl, combine cabbage, daikon, green onions, carrots and sauce. Using your hands, massage the sauce into the vegetables.

5. Press vegetables into the mason jar, squeezing until the sauce rises to cover the vegetables. Leave at least a 1-1/2-inch (4 cm) space between liquid and top of the jar. Seal with a lid.

6. Place in a flat-bottomed bowl (the kimchi may spill out) and let stand at room temperature in a dark place for 3 to 5 days, or until liquid is tangy tasting and starting to bubble slightly. Once a day, use a spoon to press down the vegetables to ensure they are submerged under the brine. Cover the jar with a lid and transfer to the fridge. Let stand in the fridge for a week before using. Store in the fridge for up to 6 months. (If any mold forms or the kimchi develops an odd aroma, throw it out.)

8-CUP (2 L) MASON JAR WITH LID

1 **medium** head napa cabbage, cut into 2-inch (5 cm) wide strips 1

1/4 **cup** sea salt 60 mL

Distilled or filtered water

4 **garlic** cloves, minced 4

1 **1/2-inch** (1 cm) piece ginger, grated 1

3 **tbsp** Korean hot pepper flakes 45 mL

1 **tbsp** vegan Worcestershire 15 mL

1 **tbsp** freshly squeezed lime juice 15 mL

1 **tsp** sugar 5 mL

1 **tsp** kelp granules 5 mL

1 **cup** matchstick-size pieces peeled daikon 250 mL

4 **green** onions, white and light green parts, cut into 1-inch (2.5 cm) pieces 4

1 **carrot,** cut into matchsticks 1

HACK IT!

You're probably wondering why distilled or filtered water is used in this recipe. Compared to tap water, both contain less chlorine, which stops food from fermenting properly.

If you love all things spicy, add 2 more tbsp (30 mL) Korean red pepper flakes.

Use kimchi to upgrade that cheap store-bought packet of ramen. Add a heaping tbsp (15 mL) to your prepared soup for a yummy, spicy, fancy twist.

Thirsty Girl

/ˈTHərstē gərl/ *noun*

1. A young woman who is dehydrated and requires a beverage.
2. A female who is eager for material gifts, monetary instruments or the gift of alcohol at a bar or nightclub. *"Cynthia's friend Monica's been getting free drinks from that rich guy all night. What a thirsty girl."*
3. A youthful lady with a need to gain admiration through social media by posting pictures of herself to boost her self-esteem, often prompting the question from her friends: *"Who the eff took this photo?!"*

WE ALL GET THIRSTY SOMETIMES — it's natural. Here is a variety of drinks to make you feel good, no matter what the occasion. Whether you're looking for a healthy breakfast or need to extend your weekend's merriment on Sunday Funday, we've got all the options to wet your whistle.

The Ginger Shot

MAKES ABOUT 3 CUPS (750 ML)

Shots! Shots! Shots! While this might be as palatable as tequila, I promise it won't make you act like you drank tequila. Your pants will remain safely on . . . *for now.* James and I drink a ginger shot every morning, along with our Mean Green Ginger Machine (page 236). It's actually the only morning routine besides coffee I've ever been able to stick to. It does wonders for the body, and it is really energizing. Some people claim they've even been able to quit their morning cup of joe. I mean, it's good, but I'm not sure it's *that* good.

1. If using a juicer, juice ginger and apples. If using a blender, blend ginger and apples on High until smooth.

2. Using a fine-mesh sieve, strain orange juice, lemon juice and ginger-apple juice into a large measuring cup or bowl.

3. Transfer to a large glass bottle or jar, add turmeric and twist on the lid. Tip the bottle over to combine. Serve immediately or store in the fridge. Enjoy as shots, or mix a shot glass or two into your fave fruit or green juice for an added kick. Spicy orange juice is the best!

JUICER OR HIGH-
POWERED BLENDER
FINE-MESH SIEVE

7 oz ginger, cut into chunks
 210 g
2 apples, cut into wedges 2
Juice of 3 oranges
Juice of 1 lemon
1 tsp ground turmeric 5 mL

HACK IT!

You'll need a chunk of ginger that's about the size of a small hand.

Add 1/4 to 1/2 tsp (1 to 2 mL) cayenne pepper to your juice for its anti-flu and digestive properties.

Add more or less fruit to make your shot fit your mood. Some days I like it pure, with just lemon and ginger, while others I love it a bit milder with more fruit juice. Get all Bob Ross on your juice.

This recipe makes enough juice to last for 5 days, so you don't have to make a pulpy mess every morning. Store in a glass container to help reduce oxidization, and pour out shots as you need them.

The Healthy Cocktail Mix

SERVES 2

When I was young (read: foolish), I believed that alcohol was less bad for you if you mixed it with something like vegetable juice. Now that I'm wise (read: old), I add vodka to my fresh juice to make it naughty. This healthful juice has a lovely citrus tang and a subtly spicy kick for when you're feeling bad.

1. If using a juicer, juice carrots and ginger. If using a blender, blend carrots and ginger on High until smooth.

2. Using a fine-mesh sieve, strain orange juice, lime juice and ginger-carrot juice into a large measuring cup or bowl.

3. Transfer to a large glass bottle or pitcher. Add the lid and shake to combine, or stir if using a pitcher. Serve immediately or store in the fridge for up to 5 days. Enjoy on its own or mix with your favorite alcohol (I like prosecco) for a guilt-free cocktail.

JUICER OR HIGH-POWERED BLENDER
FINE-MESH SIEVE

4 carrots 4
1 3-inch (7.5 cm) piece ginger 1
Juice of 6 oranges (approx. 1-1/2 cups/375 mL)
Juice of 1/2 lime

∼∼ HACK IT! ∼∼∼∼∼∼∼∼∼∼∼∼∼

Add **1/4 to 1/2 tsp** (1 to 2 mL) cayenne pepper to your juice for its anti-flu and digestive properties.

Mean Green Ginger Machine

SERVES 2

Would this be a vegan cookbook without a green smoothie of some kind? Clearly this beverage is here as a counterbalance to every fried dish in this book. Yes, it's healthy, yes, it tastes amazing, and guess what?! It helps clear out your system from chapters 2 to 7. #winning

1. In a blender, combine almond milk, matcha powder, avocado, lemon juice, banana, mango, ginger, spinach, flax seeds and maple syrup; blend on High until smooth. If the mixture is too thick, add more almond milk to help your blender process the frozen fruit.

2. Pour into a mason jar, a tumbler or a glass and enjoy.

BLENDER

2 cups unsweetened almond milk (approx.) 375 mL
1 tbsp food-grade matcha powder 15 mL
1/2 avocado 1/2
3 tbsp freshly squeezed lemon juice 45 mL
1/2 frozen banana 1/2
1 cup frozen chopped mango 250 mL
1-1/2 tsp minced fresh ginger 7 mL
2 cups spinach 500 mL
1 tbsp ground flax seeds 15 mL
2 tbsp pure maple syrup 30 mL

Mint Chocolate Chip Smoothie

SERVES 1

I am not one of those people who can blend up a bunch of healthy stuff that doesn't go together and gobble it down as a smoothie. As a rule, all food that touches these lips, whether in liquid form or not, must be tasty. Yes, I consider this cloud of minty, chocolaty heaven part of a balanced breakfast.

1. In a blender, combine almond milk, banana, cocoa powder, chlorophyll, mint extract, maple syrup, almond butter, spinach and ice; blend on High until smooth. Add cocoa nibs and blend on Low just to combine, so nibs are still slightly crunchy.

2. Pour into a mason jar, a tumbler or a glass and top with additional cocoa nibs to garnish.

 *HACK IT!*

Take this smoothie to beast mode by adding a scoop of chocolate protein powder.

Liquid chlorophyll (not to be confused with chloroform) is a great source of vitamins A, C, E and K. It can be found at your local health food store.

BLENDER

1 cup unsweetened almond milk 250 mL
1 frozen banana 1
1 tbsp unsweetened cocoa powder 15 mL
1 tbsp liquid chlorophyll 15 mL
1/2 tsp mint extract 2 mL
2 tbsp pure maple syrup 30 mL
1 tbsp smooth almond butter 15 mL
1 cup spinach 250 mL
3 ice cubes 3
2 tbsp cocoa nibs or vegan dark chocolate chips 30 mL
Additional cocoa nibs

Crispy Coffee Smoothie

SERVES 1

What if I told you that you could have a coffee, a smoothie *and* chocolate for breakfast? I know, you'd say, "Wow, Candice, you're crazy smart!" After this tasty treat, you'll wonder why you haven't been putting coffee in your smoothies all along.

1. In a blender, combine soy milk, coffee, oats, banana, cocoa powder, maple syrup, almond butter, flax seeds, vanilla and ice cubes; blend on High until smooth.

2. Pour into a mason jar, a tumbler or a glass and top with cocoa nibs, if desired.

BLENDER

3/4 cup unsweetened soy or almond milk 175 mL
1/2 cup cold brewed coffee 125 mL
1/4 cup large-flake (old-fashioned) rolled oats 60 mL
1 frozen banana 1
1 tbsp unsweetened cocoa powder 15 mL
2 tbsp pure maple syrup 30 mL
1 tbsp smooth almond butter 15 mL
1-1/2 tsp ground flax seeds 7 mL
1/2 tsp vanilla extract 2 mL
5 ice cubes 5
Cocoa nibs (optional)

Grade Eh, Caesar

SERVES 1

The Caesar is the customary Canadian hangover cure of champions. Hockey players drink it for its healing properties every morning, along with a shooter of pure maple syrup, before taking their beaver for a walk. Unlike its southern counterpart, the Bloody Mary, the Caesar uses Clamato juice (or in this case, a clam-free version made with olive juice and sauerkraut) as its rich and soothing base. Best enjoyed out of the Stanley Cup.

1. With a highball glass, take 1 lime wedge and run it round the rim. Place celery salt on a small plate. Dip the rim of the glass in celery salt. Set aside.

2. In another highball glass, cocktail shaker or measuring cup, combine tomato juice, vodka, vegan Worcestershire, lemon juice, sauerkraut, horseradish, olive juice, Tabasco and pepper to taste.

3. Fill the rimmed glass with ice, then pour in cocktail. Take a cocktail pick and string desired garnishes across the length. Place a celery stalk in the glass and garnish with lemon wedge and remaining lime wedge. Lay loaded cocktail pick across top of the glass and serve.

HACK IT!

Olive juice is a pretty weird ingredient, huh? Well, don't you worry; all you need to do is steal some from a jar of olives sitting in your fridge! Easy peasy.

HIGHBALL GLASS
COCKTAIL PICK (OPTIONAL)

2 **lime** wedges, divided 2
Celery salt for rimming
1/2 cup tomato juice 125 mL
1-1/2 oz vodka 45 mL
1 tsp vegan Worcestershire 5 mL
1 tsp freshly squeezed lemon juice 5 mL
1 tbsp white sauerkraut, finely chopped 15 mL
1 tsp prepared horseradish 5 mL
2 tbsp olive juice 30 mL
1/8 tsp Tabasco or hot sauce 0.5 mL
Freshly ground black pepper
1 cup ice cubes 250 mL
1 celery stalk 1
1 lemon wedge 1

GARNISHES
(TAKE YOUR PICK)
Pickled bean
Gherkin
Green olive
Pickled ginger
Pickled garlic or onion
Cucumber slice

Ginger Kombucha Mimosa

SERVES 8

Have you caught the kombucha fever yet? This bubbly tea drink has been called an "immortal health elixir," and it's seriously trendy in the health community. Since I truly believe in keeping a holistic and balanced approach to consuming anything, I decided to use this fermented, probiotic, carbonated potion as a cocktail mixer. Because if you add something healthy to your cocktail, it automatically makes it a health food, right?

1. In a large pitcher, combine orange juice and kombucha. Top with prosecco; stir to combine.

2. Put 3 raspberries at bottom of each champagne flute. Pour in kombucha mixture.

3. Serve.

HACK IT!

We like this mimosa with ginger kombucha, but use any flavor of kombucha your heart desires. Try using different fruit juices and fresh fruit (like blood orange!) for new and exciting cocktail combinations.

You can make any cocktail a health tonic by swapping out your traditional sugary mixer for flavored kombucha.

8 CHAMPAGNE FLUTES

3 cups freshly squeezed orange juice 750 mL

1 cup store-bought ginger-flavored kombucha 250 mL

2 cups prosecco or sparkling wine 500 mL

24 raspberries 24

Picante de la Casa

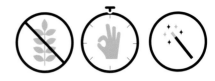

SERVES 1

I adore tequila. (I know what you're thinking. Stop cringing: Jose Cuervo doesn't count as tequila — that stuff is bottled migraine.) Good 100% agave tequila is my go-to spirit for all reasons, seasons and occasions. My life was forever changed when I had my first Soho House picante, and now it's a staple in our casa, too.

1. Rub cilantro leaves in your hands to release the flavor; add to cocktail shaker and muddle. Add chile pepper, tequila, lime juice, agave and 1 cup (250 mL) ice cubes; shake vigorously. Place 3 ice cubes in an old-fashioned glass; strain cocktail into the glass.

2. Garnish with a slice of chile pepper.

 HACK IT!

You can use any chile pepper you love, but a Fresno is ideal.

Not into spice? Just leave out the chile pepper. Want more spice? Muddle the chile pepper. The more you muddle, the spicier the cocktail!

COCKTAIL SHAKER
MUDDLER
OLD-FASHIONED GLASS

1 sprig fresh cilantro 1
1 1/4-inch (0.5 cm) piece chile pepper 1
2 oz 100% agave tequila 60 mL
2 tbsp freshly squeezed lime juice 30 mL
1 tsp agave nectar 5 mL
1 cup ice cubes 250 mL
3 ice cubes 3
Chile pepper slice

Black Lemonade

SERVES 2

Let's get this out of the way quickly: this drink is black (like my soul), and normally black foods aren't generally appealing. In this case, black lemonade is going to be your new best friend. Not only is it incredibly refreshing, and super quick and easy to whip up, it's also the perfect hangover remedy. All thanks can be tweeted to @edgyveg.

1. In a mason jar, a bottle or a pitcher, combine water, lemon juice, charcoal and maple syrup. Add the lid and shake to combine, or stir if using a pitcher. Serve immediately or store in the fridge for up to 5 days.

HACK IT!

You can easily make many variations of flavored lemonade. Try adding 1/4 tsp (1 mL) cayenne pepper or steep 1 tbsp (15 mL) dried lavender or add a splash of juiced ginger.

4-CUP (1 L) MASON JAR, BOTTLE OR PITCHER

4 cups cold water 1 L
Juice of 2 lemons
1 tsp food-grade activated charcoal powder 5 mL
2 tbsp pure maple syrup 30 mL

Sweet Endings...
or Beginnings – We Don't Judge

/swēt ˈendiNG/   *noun*

1. An enjoyable closing or final part of something, such as a period of time, event or meal • *"This last semester was a sweet ending to my destitute yet satisfying college career."*

2. A delightful treat made with sugar, chocolate and/or whipped cream • *"Would you care to see our dessert menu? No meal is complete without a sweet ending."*

3. Foods reminiscent of — or leading to — romantic pleasure • *"The crème brûlée wasn't the only sweet ending for my date last night, if you know what I'm sayin'. . . "*

LIKE A SUCCESSFUL FIRST DATE, every great meal deserves a sweet ending. In this chapter you will find my favorite easy, go-to desserts. Perfect for high tea (read: wine) with your gal pals or to impress your mother-in-law. Lea, this one's for you!

Sponge Cake and Berries Fit for Royal Tea

SERVES 6

Victoria sponge cake is an old English classic. It's named after Queen Victoria, who apparently had tea with delectable cakes every day at four o'clock with a duchess and baroness. I do the same thing, but I swap out the tea for wine and eat cake with my dogs. So go ahead and throw an afternoon tea party with some pals, *human or canine*.

1. **Cake:** In a stand mixer bowl or large bowl, using a fine-mesh sieve, sift flour, baking powder, sea salt, baking soda and sugar. Whisk and set aside.

2. In a medium bowl, whisk together almond milk, vegetable oil, agave nectar, apple cider vinegar and vanilla.

3. Add almond milk mixture to flour mixture. Using a stand mixer with the paddle attachment or an electric hand mixer, beat for about 2 minutes, until thick and creamy.

4. Divide batter between prepared springform pans. Bake for 25 to 35 minutes, watching carefully, until golden brown and a tester inserted in the center comes out clean.

5. Remove cakes from oven and let cool in the pans for 15 minutes. Remove from the pans and transfer to a wire rack. Let cool completely, about 1 hour.

6. **Chantilly Cream:** Meanwhile, chill the clean stand mixer bowl and the whip attachment, or a large metal bowl and electric beaters, in the fridge for 1 hour.

7. Remove the cold bowl and beaters from the fridge. Carefully open coconut milk and place the coconut cream solids in the cold bowl. (Reserve or discard the remaining liquid. You do not want any of this liquid in your whipped cream.)

8. Using the stand mixer or electric hand mixer with chilled beaters, beat coconut cream on Low, gradually turning up the speed to High, for about 30 seconds to 1 minute. Beat on High for 3 to 5 minutes, until stiff peaks form. Add confectioners' sugar, vanilla, tapioca starch and cognac; beat for 1 minute, until stiff peaks form again (they can fall when new ingredients are added). Taste and adjust sugar and cognac to desired sweetness. Cover and transfer to the fridge until needed.

PREHEAT OVEN TO 350°F (180°C)
FINE-MESH SIEVE
STAND MIXER OR ELECTRIC HAND MIXER
TWO 9-INCH (23 CM) SPRINGFORM PANS, GREASED AND DUSTED WITH UNBLEACHED ALL-PURPOSE FLOUR

CAKE
2-3/4 cups unbleached all-purpose flour 675 mL
4-1/2 tsp baking powder 22 mL
1 tsp sea salt 5 mL
1-1/4 tsp baking soda 6 mL
1-1/4 cups superfine sugar 300 mL
1-2/3 cups unsweetened almond milk 400 mL
1/2 cup vegetable oil 125 mL
3 tbsp agave nectar 45 mL
2 tsp apple cider vinegar 10 mL
2 tsp vanilla extract, divided 10 mL

CHANTILLY CREAM
2 cans (each 14 oz/398 mL) full-fat coconut milk, refrigerated overnight 2
1/2 cup organic confectioners' (icing) sugar (approx.) 125 mL
2 tsp vanilla extract 10 mL
1 tbsp tapioca starch 15 mL
1 tbsp cognac (approx.) 15 mL

FILLING AND TOPPING
1/4 cup strawberry jam 60 mL
4 cups strawberries, halved 1 L

9. Place one cake on a serving dish or cake stand. Spread jam evenly over the surface, followed by half of the whipped cream, leaving a 1/2-inch (1 cm) border. Place second cake on top. Spread or pipe remaining cream over surface and decorate with strawberries. Transfer to the fridge for a minimum of 1 hour and maximum overnight to set.

10. Slice with a sharp knife and a light hand. Serve with afternoon tea or prosecco.

HACK IT!

Easily change the look and taste of this delectable cake by using a variety of berries and fresh fruit.

Make an extra-fluffy cream center by piping small, even dollops of Chantilly Cream all around inside of bottom cake, leaving a 1/2-inch (1 cm) border.

New York Cheesecake with Raspberry Coulis

SERVES 8 TO 10

Cheesecake is made of two things I love — cheese and cake. Pair this with our Steaks with Béarnaise Sauce (page 188) for the ultimate vegan New York steakhouse experience. Overpriced Merlot sold separately.

1. **Cheesecake:** Remove bottom of a springform pan. Trace an outline of bottom on a piece of parchment paper. Cut out, reassemble springform pan and line bottom with the piece of parchment. Cut out a long piece of parchment the height of your springform pan and line the inside edge of the ring.

2. In a food processor, combine almond flour, oats, coconut sugar and 1/2 tsp (2 mL) sea salt; pulse to combine. With the motor running, pour in maple syrup and melted butter through the feed tube in a steady drizzle; process until combined, and the mixture is the consistency of coarse crumbs.

3. Press mixture into bottom and up sides of the prepared pan. Bake for 10 minutes, until slightly golden brown. Set aside to cool while you prepare cake filling.

4. In a blender, combine tofu, coconut oil, apple cider vinegar, lemon juice and vanilla; blend on High until smooth, scraping down the sides, as needed. Set aside.

5. Carefully open coconut milk. Place the coconut cream solids in a stand mixer or mixing bowl. (Reserve or discard the remaining liquid. You do not want any of this liquid in your cake.) Add sugar, egg replacer, lemon zest, cornstarch and the remaining 1/2 tsp (2 mL) sea salt. Beat on Low, gradually turning up speed to High, for about 30 seconds to 1 minute. Cream on High for 2 to 3 minutes, until fluffy and creamy. Add tofu mixture and cream together for 3 to 5 minutes, until fluffy, scraping down the sides of the bowl with a rubber spatula if necessary. Taste and adjust flavor as needed: add more sugar for sweetness, apple cider vinegar for acidity or zest for tartness.

PREHEAT OVEN TO 350°F (180°C)
9-INCH (23 CM) SPRING-FORM PAN
FOOD PROCESSOR
HIGH-POWERED BLENDER
STAND MIXER OR ELECTRIC HAND MIXER
FINE-MESH SIEVE

CHEESECAKE

3 cups almond flour 750 mL

1 cup gluten-free large-flake (old-fashioned) rolled oats 250 mL

1/2 cup coconut sugar 125 mL

1 tsp sea salt, divided 5 mL

3 tbsp pure maple syrup 45 mL

1/2 cup vegan butter, melted 125 mL

2 packages (each 12 oz/340 g) soft silken tofu, drained 2

1 tbsp softened coconut oil 15 mL

3 tbsp apple cider vinegar (approx.) 45 mL

2 tbsp freshly squeezed lemon juice 30 mL

1 tbsp vanilla extract 15 mL

1 can (14 oz/398 mL) full-fat coconut milk, refrigerated overnight 1

1 cup organic sugar (approx.) 250 mL

2 tbsp powdered egg replacer (I like Ener-G) 30 mL

2 tsp grated lemon zest (approx.) 10 mL

1/3 cup cornstarch 75 mL

RASPBERRY COULIS (page 256)

6. Pour filling over prepared crust. Tap the pan on the edge of counter to remove any air bubbles. Bake in preheated oven for 60 to 70 minutes, until the edges are set and center has a slight wiggle.

7. Turn off heat and let the cheesecake sit in the oven with the door cracked for 1 hour. Remove from oven and let cool completely on a wire rack for 3 hours. DO NOT SKIP THIS STEP. Gently cover with plastic wrap and refrigerate overnight.

8. **Raspberry Coulis:** In a food processor, combine thawed raspberries, sugar and water; pulse until puréed. Be careful not to overblend: you don't want the seeds to break down small enough to pass through a sieve. Using a spatula, push raspberry purée through a fine-mesh sieve into a medium saucepan.

9. Heat raspberry purée over medium heat for about 20 minutes, whisking constantly, until slightly thickened. Add lemon juice and whisk until smooth. Remove from heat and let cool completely, about 1 hour.

10. Spoon raspberry coulis over cheesecake and arrange fresh raspberries on top, if using. Refrigerate for 1 hour to help the sauce thicken, or until ready to serve.

11. Run a knife around the edges of the pan and gently remove sides. Serve immediately.

HACK IT!

Even the most seasoned bakers sometimes get cracks in their cheesecake. It happens — just cover it with topping and no one will ever know.

This is a super-easy blank-canvas cheesecake. You can top it with any fruit your heart desires or with Chantilly Cream (page 252), Caramel Sauce (page 264) or Chocolate Sauce (page 264). Heck, you could do all three!

Cake can be left in the fridge for up to 3 days, but it is best served fresh.

RASPBERRY COULIS
1-1/2 lbs frozen raspberries, thawed 750 g
1 cup organic sugar 250 mL
3 tbsp water 45 mL
2 tbsp freshly squeezed lemon juice 30 mL
Fresh raspberries (optional)

Death by Chocolate Mousse

SERVES 4

It's no secret that in our house the only thing that disappears faster than iPhone cables is chocolate (not that I would recommend eating iPhone cables). This light, airy and yet somehow rich chocolate mousse is our #1 most misplaced item. Need a super-easy but super-fancy treat to impress your in-laws? Bingo!

1. Place chocolate chips in a wide, shallow, microwave-safe bowl. Melt in microwave at 20-second intervals, stirring between heatings. Repeat until chocolate has a smooth consistency. Set aside to cool completely, but not stiffen, while you prepare the rest of the recipe. (Just check on it once in a while. If it does stiffen, you can put it in the microwave again for 20 seconds and let it cool. Hot chocolate will ruin this mousse.)

2. In a stand mixer bowl or a large bowl, combine aquafaba and cream of tartar. Using the stand mixer or an electric hand mixer, beat on Low, gradually turning up speed to High, for about 30 seconds to 1 minute. Beat on High for about 15 minutes, until stiff peaks form. Invert the bowl: if you see the peaks sliding and moving, keep on beating until they become so stiff they don't move at all. With the mixer running, slowly add sugar and 1 tsp (5 mL) vanilla; beat for about 3 minutes, until stiff peaks form again. Drizzle chocolate into aquafaba mixture and gently fold in with a spatula, until well combined.

3. Evenly divide mixture between four mason jars, individual trifle cups or ramekins. Transfer to the fridge to set for at least 3 hours, but overnight is best.

4. Chill the clean stand mixer bowl, or a large metal bowl and electric beaters, in the fridge for 1 hour.

5. Carefully open coconut milk. Place coconut cream solids in cold bowl. (Reserve or discard the remaining liquid. You do not want any of this liquid in your whipped cream.)

6. Using the stand mixer or the electric hand mixer with chilled beaters, beat coconut cream on Low, gradually turning up speed to High, for about 30 seconds to 1 minute. Beat on High for about 3 to 5 minutes, until stiff

STAND MIXER OR ELECTRIC HAND MIXER
FOUR 1-CUP (250 ML) WIDE-MOUTH MASON JARS, INDIVIDUAL TRIFLE CUPS OR RAMEKINS

1-1/2 cups vegan dark chocolate chips 375 mL
1 cup aquafaba 250 mL
1/4 tsp cream of tartar 1 mL
1 tbsp organic sugar 15 mL
2 tsp vanilla extract, divided 10 mL
1 can (14 oz/398 mL) full-fat coconut milk, refrigerated overnight 1
1/4 cup organic confectioners' (icing) sugar (approx.) 60 mL
1 tbsp tapioca starch 15 mL
Vegan chocolate shavings or cocoa nibs (optional)
Sliced almonds (optional)

peaks form. Add confectioners' sugar, 1 tsp (5 mL) vanilla and tapioca starch; beat for 1 minute. Taste and add more confectioners' sugar, if necessary. Cover and transfer to the fridge until needed and for up to 3 days.

7. Spoon whipped cream over top of set mousse. Top with chocolate shavings, cocoa nibs and/or sliced almonds; serve.

HACK IT!

I like to have a little fun with the presentation. I use tall serving cups or glass tea cups and place them at an angle inside an egg carton or bowl, leaning it against the edge, which makes the mousse set at an angle, too. Pipe some whipped cream on top after the mousse has set and add some chocolate shavings as garnish.

You can use the unused liquid from the coconut milk in smoothies or cocktails, or just drink it straight.

This mousse and cream will firm when chilled and soften at room temperature, so don't let it sit out for too long. Keep in the fridge for up to 3 days.

You MUST use good-quality, full-fat coconut milk for this recipe to work. I find that I have the most success with this recipe when using Thai Kitchen or Whole Foods 365 Everyday Value brand. They create a nice thick coconut cream, as they have a higher proportion of fat than other brands.

"Literally Dying" Skillet Cookie à la Mode

SERVES 6 TO 8

Sometimes bigger *is* better. Case in point — this crunchy-on-the-outside, creamy-on-the-inside giant cookie.

1. In a large bowl, whisk together flour, baking powder and sea salt. Set aside.

2. In another large bowl, whisk together light brown sugar and organic sugar. Add melted butter. Using a wooden spoon, mix until smooth.

3. In a small bowl, whisk together egg replacer, water and vanilla. Add vanilla mixture to sugar mixture; stir until smooth.

4. Add flour mixture to the sugar mixture. Using a wooden spoon, stir until well combined. Fold in chocolate chips and spread evenly in a skillet.

5. Bake in preheated oven for 30 minutes, until edges are golden brown and center looks slightly loose. Do not overcook.

6. Place the skillet on a wire rack and let cool for 15 minutes. (No one wants to burn the roof of their mouth.) Slice like a pizza and top with a scoop of ice cream.

7. Scoop the gooey deliciousness onto plates or bowls, or eat directly from the skillet, like I do!

PREHEAT OVEN TO 350°F (180°C)
10-INCH (25 CM) OVEN-SAFE SKILLET, CAST IRON PREFERRED

2 cups unbleached all-purpose flour 500 mL

1-1/2 tsp baking powder 7 mL

1/4 tsp sea salt 1 mL

1 cup packed light brown sugar 250 mL

1/2 cup organic sugar 125 mL

3/4 cup melted vegan butter 175 mL

2 tbsp powdered egg replacer (I like Ener-G) 30 mL

6 tbsp water 90 mL

2 tsp vanilla extract 10 mL

1 cup vegan semisweet chocolate chips 250 mL

1 recipe Vanilla Ice Cream, Baby (page 267) 1

HACK IT!

I love to reduce the chocolate chips by half and add 1/2 cup (125 mL) crushed walnuts to the cookie dough. Yummy! Try adding your favorite nuts to change up this crowd-pleaser.

This dough also makes awesome normal-size cookies. Spoon 1 tbsp (15 mL) per cookie onto a baking sheet lined with parchment paper and bake for 15 minutes, until light brown.

Since this is a vegan recipe, you can eat this cookie dough raw. Have it on its own or add to vanilla ice cream to make homemade chocolate chip cookie–dough ice cream.

Crème Brûlée All Day

SERVES 4

Ah yes, crème brûlée, or "burnt cream," for those of us who don't speak *le français*. This classic dessert is a symphony of luscious cream and sweet vanilla that most of us would never dare to try at home. But really, crème brûlée is just egg custard with a hard, sugary crust. You can pull this off no problem! Use this to wow any fancy dinner guest. It takes just a few minutes to prepare, and you get to use a blowtorch!!! #CremeBruleeAllDay

1. **Custard:** Carefully open coconut milk. Place 1 cup (250 mL) coconut cream solids in a medium saucepan. Make sure you don't get any liquid in your coconut milk solids. (Reserve or discard the remaining liquid.)

2. In a small bowl, whisk together almond milk and corn-starch. Set aside.

3. Heat the medium saucepan over medium-high heat and whisk together coconut milk solids, sugar, nutritional yeast and sea salt, just until simmering but not boiling. Immediately reduce heat to medium-low and slowly drizzle in the cornstarch mixture; cook, whisking continuously, for about 5 minutes, until very thick. Remove from heat and whisk in vanilla.

4. Pour mixture evenly into ramekins and smooth the tops, using a spatula or a spoon. Let cool for 10 minutes.

5. **Topping:** Sprinkle 2 tsp (10 mL) sugar over the top of each custard. Give the ramekin a little shake to spread out the sugar evenly.

6. With the torch at full blast, holding it about 3 inches (7.5 cm) from the surface of the custard, move the flame back and forth to melt the sugar until it bubbles and turns slightly golden. (Be sure to move your torch constantly or else you will end up with burnt sugar.) Repeat with the remaining custards. Let crème brûlée cool for 3 minutes, then serve.

FOUR 4-1/2 OZ (135 ML)
RAMEKINS
KITCHEN TORCH

CUSTARD
2 cans (14 oz/398 mL) full-fat coconut milk, refrigerated overnight 2
2/3 cup unsweetened almond milk 150 mL
1/4 cup cornstarch 60 mL
1/3 cup organic sugar 75 mL
1 tsp nutritional yeast 5 mL
Sea salt
1 tsp vanilla extract 5 mL

TOPPING
8 tsp organic sugar, divided 40 mL

～ HACK IT! ～

For a richer vanilla flavor, replace vanilla extract with the seeds and pod of 1 vanilla bean. Scrape out the seeds and add the pod to the mixture when cooking. Discard pod.

For an extra-thick crackly top, after browning the sugar in Step 6, add 2 tsp (10 mL) more sugar to each custard and repeat the torching process a second time.

Sundaes Are for Millionaires

MAKES 9 SMALL OR 4 LARGE SQUARES

What do you call a buttery shortbread crust topped with velvety vanilla ice cream and caramel and chocolate drizzle? I couldn't decide whether it was an ice-cream cake or an open-face ice-cream sandwich, so it became a sundae. I'm a millennial, so I don't like labels.

1. **Shortbread Crust:** Using a stand mixer or an electric hand mixer, cream together butter and sugar for about 2 minutes, until light and fluffy.

2. In a large bowl, whisk together flour, baking powder and salt.

3. With the mixer on low speed, slowly add flour mixture, almond milk and vanilla to butter mixture, beating until a soft dough forms.

4. Press dough into prepared pan. Cover with plastic wrap and refrigerate for about 15 minutes, until dough is as firm as a stick of butter.

5. Bake for 20 to 22 minutes, until slightly golden in color. Remove from the oven and let cool completely in the pan, or else you will end up with a hot mess of soggy melted ice-cream goo.

6. **Caramel Sauce:** Meanwhile, in a small saucepan, bring sugar, water and maple syrup to a boil over medium-high heat. Boil for 5 minutes, whisking to dissolve the sugar and prevent burning. Reduce heat to low and simmer for about 10 to 15 minutes, stirring occasionally, until syrup is deep amber. Remove from heat and stir in coconut milk, butter and sea salt to taste, until well combined. Let cool slightly.

7. Spread ice cream over shortbread. Drizzle caramel sauce across the top and transfer to the freezer. Freeze until hardened completely, for at least 4 hours or up to overnight.

8. **Chocolate Sauce:** Place chocolate chips in a microwave-safe bowl and microwave at 30-second intervals until melted, stirring between heatings. Add coconut oil and mix until melted and well combined. You may need to return the bowl to your microwave for a few seconds, to ensure it all melts evenly.

9. Remove the pan from the freezer and let stand for 5 minutes. Slice into bars and drizzle with chocolate sauce. Serve immediately.

PREHEAT OVEN TO 350°F (180°C)
STAND MIXER OR ELECTRIC HAND MIXER
8-INCH (20 CM) SQUARE METAL PAN LINED WITH PARCHMENT PAPER

SHORTBREAD CRUST
1 cup softened vegan butter 250 mL
1/2 cup organic sugar 125 mL
2 cups unbleached all-purpose flour 500 mL
1/2 tsp baking powder 2 mL
1/2 tsp salt 2 mL
2 tbsp unsweetened almond milk 30 mL
1/2 tsp vanilla extract 2 mL

CARAMEL SAUCE
1 cup organic sugar 250 mL
1/4 cup water 60 mL
2 tbsp pure maple syrup 30 mL
1/4 cup full-fat canned coconut milk 60 mL
1 tbsp vegan butter 15 mL
Sea salt

1 recipe Vanilla Ice Cream, Baby (page 267) 1

CHOCOLATE SAUCE
1/2 cup vegan dark chocolate chips 125 mL
1-1/2 tsp coconut oil 7 mL

Vanilla Ice Cream, Baby

MAKES 4 CUPS (1 L)

Ah, ice cream. One of the most iconic foods that most people think can't be made vegan (or made vegan well). This smooth, rich and creamy vanilla ice cream will make a believer out of even the harshest skeptics and put a happy smile on just about anyone, even, say, a white '90s one-hit-wonder rapper.

1. Carefully open coconut milk. Place coconut cream solids in a small saucepan. (Reserve or discard the remaining liquid. You do not want any of this liquid in your ice cream.) Scrape vanilla seeds and pod into the saucepan (or pour in extract) and add sugar and a pinch of sea salt. Bring to a simmer over medium heat, whisking constantly, until sugar dissolves, about 10 minutes. Remove from heat. If using vanilla bean, cover and let stand for 30 minutes. Discard pod.

2. In a blender, combine cashews and almond milk; blend on High until thick and creamy. Add coconut milk mixture and blend until very smooth.

3. Pour mixture into an ice-cream maker. Churn until cream has thickened to a consistency similar to soft-serve. In most ice-cream makers, this takes about 25 minutes — check the instructions for your machine.

4. Serve immediately or prepare to freeze. Transfer to a freezer container and press a piece of wax paper against the surface to prevent ice crystals from forming. Freeze for about 4 hours, until solid.

HACK IT!

The ice cream will keep in the freezer for 2 weeks before becoming icy.

HIGH-POWERED BLENDER ICE-CREAM MAKER

2 cans (each 14 oz/398 mL) full-fat coconut milk, refrigerated overnight 2

1 vanilla bean, split lengthwise (or 1-1/2 tsp/7 mL vanilla extract) 1

3/4 cup organic sugar 175 mL

Sea salt

1 cup raw cashews, soaked overnight and rinsed (see page 26) 250 mL

1/2 cup unsweetened almond milk 125 mL

I Can Haz Strawberry Ice Cream?

MAKES 3 CUPS (750 ML)

. . . Yes, yes, you can. I spent many summers in the fields of rural Ontario picking strawberries with my sisters. It was hard work, but man oh man, did we get great tans! This velvety pink ice cream is brought to you by sun on my shoulders and summertime happiness.

1. In a large bowl, using a potato masher or a fork, coarsely mash together strawberries, sugar, lemon juice and sea salt. Let stand for 15 minutes, stirring and mashing occasionally.

2. Carefully open coconut milk. Place coconut milk solids in a blender. (Reserve or discard the remaining liquid. You do not want any of this liquid in your ice cream.) Add cashews, almond milk and vanilla; blend on High until thick and creamy. Set aside.

3. Transfer half the strawberry mixture to the blender. Blend on High until smooth. Pour strawberry cream purée into bowl with the remaining strawberries; stir until well combined.

4. Pour mixture into an ice-cream maker. Churn until mixture has thickened to a consistency similar to soft-serve. In most ice-cream makers, this takes about 25 minutes — check the instructions for your machine.

5. Serve immediately or prepare to freeze. Transfer to a freezer container and press a piece of wax paper against the surface of the ice cream, which will prevent ice crystals from forming. Freeze for at least 4 hours, until solid.

HIGH-POWERED BLENDER
POTATO MASHER
(OPTIONAL)
ICE-CREAM MAKER

1 lb strawberries, halved 500 g
3/4 cup organic sugar 175 mL
3/4 tsp freshly squeezed lemon juice 3 mL
1/8 tsp sea salt 0.5 mL
1 can (14 oz/398 mL) full-fat coconut milk, refrigerated overnight 1
1 cup raw cashews, soaked overnight and rinsed (see page 26) 250 mL
1/2 cup unsweetened almond milk 125 mL
1 tsp vanilla extract 5 mL

HACK IT!

You must use high-quality full-fat coconut milk, not low-fat. It's the key to luscious, creamy ice cream.

The ice cream will keep in the freezer for about 2 weeks before becoming icy.

Thank You Very Matcha Ice Cream

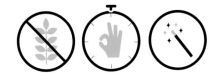

MAKES 3 CUPS (750 ML)

I read once that Buddhist monks drink matcha for its potential to heighten concentration and enhance metabolism. So here's my theory: if matcha is healthy, and matcha's in my ice cream . . . then that means — and I'm no mathematician — that ice cream is good for you?! Now, that's *my* idea of the perfect Netflix-and-chill.

1. In a blender, combine cashews and almond milk. Blend on High until thick and creamy. Measure out 2 cups (500 mL) coconut milk solids and add to blender. (Reserve or discard the remaining liquid. You do not want any of this liquid in your ice cream.) Add sugar, vanilla, matcha and a pinch of sea salt and blend until very smooth and creamy.

2. Pour mixture into an ice-cream maker. Churn until mixture has thickened to a consistency similar to soft-serve. In most ice-cream makers, this takes about 25 minutes — check the instructions for your machine.

3. Serve immediately or prepare to freeze. Transfer to a freezer container and press a piece of wax paper against the surface of the ice cream, which will prevent ice crystals from forming. Freeze for at least 4 hours, until solid.

HIGH-POWERED BLENDER
ICE-CREAM MAKER

1 cup raw cashews, soaked overnight and rinsed (see page 26) 250 mL
1/2 cup unsweetened almond milk 125 mL
3 cans (each 14 oz/398 mL) full-fat coconut milk, refrigerated overnight 3
3/4 cup organic sugar 175 mL
1 tsp vanilla extract 5 mL
2 tbsp food-grade matcha powder 30 mL
Sea salt

HACK IT!

Add more or less matcha, depending on how strong you want the flavor to be. Taste-test along the way until you're happy with the flavor. You can also pull back on the sugar and vanilla for a less sweet, more vibrant green tea flavor.

Use food-grade matcha for cooking and baking. It's half the price, and you can't tell the difference.

The ice cream will keep in the freezer for about 2 weeks before becoming icy.

Acknowledgments

What's the saying? It takes a village? This book DID take a village, especially because we wanted to bring it to the world in such a short amount of time. I have to be honest, I never thought this was going to be possible. I definitely need to express my gratitude to the many people who made this book possible. A huge thank-you:

To my amazing styling and photography team: Camille Stone, for the long hours spent finding the perfect props and creating visual styles and color palettes for our food to look amazing, and for having more patience than I could ever have asked for. You truly are a godsend, and I will be forever grateful. Spencer Shields, for spending six weeks in studio with a group of women and letting us torture you while you prepped, cooked and plated all my annoying requests to make our recipes look more beautiful than I ever could. Photographer Brilynn Ferguson, for capturing the madness and turning every recipe in this book into a work of art through your lens, and always indulging my wacky ideas. *Our next book idea shall be — smashed and melting ice cream!* Tyler and Laura at Still Life Props for their generous help providing props for each dish. Designer Walter Green, for the gorgeous and unique design that makes our words and recipes pop on every single page.

To Robert Dees and Meredith Dees from Robert Rose, for taking a chance on us and making this book possible, not to mention the endless hours of editing to get everything just right. The rest of the Robert Rose team; Kelly Glover, Marian Jarkovich, Martine Quibell, Nina McCreath, Kevin Cockburn, both Jennifers (MacKenzie and Foster) and some behind-the-scenes folks I'm sure I missed, for introducing us to the book industry, being our biggest cheerleaders, and making sure that every recipe makes sense. Thanks for thinking of a million things I would never have thought to think of. You've taught me many lessons and made me realize I still have a lot to learn.

To my family: My mother, Michaela Hutchings, for teaching me about compassion for all living creatures and always pushing me to be fearless and do good in the world even if no one else agrees. My father, for being my biggest fan no matter what strange project I took on. My mother-in-law and grandmother-in-law, Lea Barclay and Leyla Aita, for their awesome recipe contributions and inspiration. To my Omi and Opa (Renate and Albrecht) for giving me a passion for cooking and providing me with an insatiable palate for fresh ingredients. All of you are responsible for creating two insatiable food monsters. Thank you for all the meals we've shared, the kitchen dance parties, the culinary arguments and fails, and the numerous desserts we've indulged in.

To our friends: Specifically, Ashley Hubley, Alex Johnson, Dave Gicza, Ruth Thornbury, Peter Juretic, Olga Movtchan, Andrew Campbell and many others along the way who spent long hours waiting for dinner every night to taste and re-taste all the recipes in this book at our family breakfasts, lunches and dinners. And, of course, to Ryan Thomas Woods, my other true love, and bestie for keeping me calm, on track and focused when the world seemed to be falling around me.

To the many chefs who have inspired me over the years: Anthony Bourdain, David Chang, Alton Brown, Grant Achatz, Julia Child, Massimo Bottura, Isa Chandra Moskowitz and Miyoko Schinner — thank you for what you have contributed to the culinary landscape, and to my personal obsession for the perfect dish.

To our YouTube community and all of the Edgy Veg subscriber family! Thank you for all your continued support and kind words and for pushing us to be the best versions of ourselves daily. We love you, Veg Fam!

Last and not least: my husband, James. Thank you for your patience, your double- and sometimes triple-hour workdays writing this book with me. For the many trips to Whole Foods and various Asian markets, day in and day out, and for *trying* to keep me sane. Thank you for choosing to continue to love me during the toughest parts of this book-writing process, for letting me feed you questionable vegan food, and for providing me with a space to share my passion for compassion, and for indulging me in my quest to save all the animals. I promise I will *try* to sleep at least eight hours a night now.

I beg forgiveness of all those who have been with me over the years and whose names I have failed to mention, but who have inspired, supported, and helped this all be possible.

Index

Index

Index

Index

Index

Index

Index

Index

About The Edgy Veg

Candice Hutchings is the host of *The Edgy Veg* YouTube channel (250,000+ subscribers and counting) and blog, which she co-founded with her husband, James Aita. The couple live in Toronto, Ontario, with their two dogs, Sir Winston Churchill and Harley Quinn (@vedgydogs).

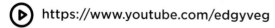

▶ https://www.youtube.com/edgyveg

📷 @edgyveg

f facebook.com/theedgyveg

🐦 @edgyveg

For more recipe inspo and videos visit us at
www.theedgyveg.com